GOLFING GREATS

GREAT BRITAIN & IRELAND

GORDON SIMPSON

SPORTSPRINT PUBLISHING
EDINBURGH

For my grandfather, James Elliot, my non-sporting hero.

ISBN 0 85976 283 1

Phototypeset by Newtext Composition Ltd., Glasgow
Printed in Great Britain by
Bell & Bain Ltd., Glasgow

ACKNOWLEDGEMENTS

My special thanks to the various golfers who co-operated so willingly in this project. Talking to them about their careers was a pleasure. I am also indebted to several others for their assistance, namely Mrs Eunice Rees, Mrs Joan Brown, John Panton, Alex Lyle, Brian Huggett and Peter Oosterhuis. Thanks to the staff of *Golf Monthly*, to Aberdeen Journals for pictorial help, to photographer Phil Sheldon for the colour material and particularly to D.C. Thomson for providing the majority of the black and white photos.

CONTENTS

INTRODUCTION

DARKNESS had descended on Augusta National Golf Club as the final putt disappeared into the hole. The television camera peered through the murky gloom and lingered on a tall, inscrutable Englishman.

Nick Faldo rocked back on his heels, threw his arms towards the leaden skies exultantly and stood in open-mouthed, wide-eyed disbelief as the enormity of his achievement sunk in.

Some 20 minutes later a kilted Scotsman sporting a green jacket slipped an identical garment over the shoulders of his English successor as U.S. Masters champion. Sandy Lyle congratulated Faldo and set the seal on arguably the most significant moment in British professional golf since the Second World War — positive proof, if it was needed, that America had forfeited its claim to be regarded as the sport's master race.

Sandy Lyle and Nick Faldo may never become the firmest of friends; their rivalry over the greater part of 20 years has been too intense, too often touched by acrimony, to allow genuine warmth to thaw their frosty relationship.

Yet that simmering rivalry between two contrasting individuals has been the catalyst in British golf's gradual revival in recent years. Lyle's Open Championship triumph in 1985 drove Faldo to emulate that achievement two years later.

Then after the Scot had become the first Briton to be measured for the green jacket, the Englishman required only 12 months more to level the score at two 'majors' apiece.

It was not until the 52nd Masters championship that Britain could acclaim a winner when big, solid, dependable Sandy Lyle produced the bunker shot of a lifetime to capture the title in 1988.

Exactly one year later, Lyle beat a hasty retreat from the Masters after missing the halfway cut, but Faldo hung around long enough to overcome a third-round stumble and assume the mantle of champion with his memorable play-off success over Scott Hoch.

The sight of two Britons — one an affable, uncomplicated Scot and the other a complex, sensitive Englishman — wearing the coveted green jackets would have seemed preposterous some years ago. But no longer.

Faldo's success represented the fifth occasion that the Masters title had been spirited away to Europe during the eighties, a decade in which golf on this side of the Atlantic truly came of age.

Henry Cotton, charismatic, sophisticated and utterly single-minded in his pursuit of excellence, had repelled the overseas raiders half a century earlier by winning the Open Championship three times. Then since the decline of the man known reverentially as 'The Maestro', several British golfers have attempted to emulate those achievements.

Fred Daly, the solitary Irishman to win the Open title, and the gifted but eccentric Englishman Max Faulkner both succeeded up to a point. They captured the Open once, but could not become multiple winners of major championships.

Tony Jacklin did precisely that in 1969 and '70 and his victories in the British and American Opens pioneered the way for a new generation of tougher, hungrier, and technically proficient players. Crucially, those players no longer considered themselves as inferior to their rich, boastful cousins in the United States.

Jacklin's role in the renaissance of British golf is a key one. An outstandingly talented player, he arrived on the professional scene when it called for a new Messiah, someone to defend British honour against the might of Uncle Sam; a golfer capable of taking on and beating virtual deities like Arnold Palmer and Jack Nicklaus.

It was a challenge he tackled with almost obsessive enthusiasm and Jacklin eventually ended 18 years of foreign domination by lifting the Open title at Royal Lytham in 1969. That same year, Jacklin affirmed his position as the new golfing hero by helping Britain and Ireland to a breathtaking halved match with America in the Ryder Cup at Birkdale.

The meeting of the two golfing superpowers went down in Ryder Cup history as one of the most dramatic confrontations since Manchester seed merchant Samuel Ryder donated a £250 gold trophy to be played for on a bi-annual basis in 1927.

The match also provided one shining example of true golfing greatness. Appropriately, the central figure was Jack Nicklaus, whose sporting ethos demands that scrupulous fair-play, humility and dignity are as vital to the game as aptitude and application.

As a titanic struggle reached its climax, little Brian Huggett holed a treacherous four and a half foot putt on the last green to halve with Billy Casper. The fiery Welsh terrier was convinced he needed the putt to win the Ryder Cup and dissolved in tears as captain Eric Brown threw a protective arm around Huggett in a comforting gesture.

Jacklin then needed to halve his tie with Nicklaus to ensure that the match was shared. The American got down safely in par, leaving Jacklin a teasing two footer to do the same. He didn't need to try.

As the Golden Bear holed out, he picked up Jacklin's marker. 'I don't think you would have missed that one, Tony,' he said. 'But I didn't want to give you the chance.'

It was a remarkably generous gesture (and by no means unanimously approved of in the American camp), which typified a player who has enriched British golf with his presence on these shores for more than a quarter of a century.

Lee Trevino, one of the few golfers in the post-war era to make a successful defence of his British Open title, once wrote: 'There is nothing quite like playing in the British Isles. Golf is in the air there. You breathe it, like smelling home cooking. It makes you hungry. You want to play.'

Nicklaus endorsed those sentiments, managing to combine his enormous talent with a perceptive understanding of the traditions and history of the Royal and Ancient game. Even when things went horribly wrong, he escaped with his dignity and reputation intact.

Unlike many American professionals today, Nicklaus patronised the Open from the moment he left the amateur ranks, but occasionally the fickle British weather soured the love affair.

In 1981 at Sandwich — Nicklaus's least favourite Open venue — he shot an 83 in the most foul conditions and immediately dropped out of contention. A small côterie of reporters decided the story was still worth recording.

Cold, wet, angry and humiliated, Nicklaus was a Golden Bear with a sore head as the interview commenced. 'So how'd you feel about your 83, Jack?' demanded his hard-nosed interrogator.

'How would you feel if you'd shot 83?' asked Nicklaus testily. 'I don't know . . . I've never shot an 83!' retorted the quick witted hack. Even Nicklaus failed to suppress a smile.

As an American, there is no place for Nicklaus in this book, but his influence pervaded two British households in the late sixties and early seventies and inspired the eighties boom.

Sandy Lyle attended the 1969 Open as an 11-year-old schoolboy and rushed home to his father and announced: 'I want to be like Nicklaus and Palmer.'

Similarly, Nick Faldo was allowed to sit up late during the 1971 Easter holidays . . . and marvelled at the kaleidoscope of colour created by the banks of azaleas and dogwood at Augusta National. Charles Coody won that Masters . . . but Jack Nicklaus was the man who caught the eye and fired the imagination of the impressionable teenager.

Just as Lyle had been captivated two years previously, sports-mad Faldo was hooked and also informed his parents: 'I think I'd like to try that golf.' Eighteen years later both Britons had reached the pinnacle of professional golf and won 'majors' on both sides of the ocean.

The emergence of Lyle and Faldo coincided with the decision to throw open the Ryder Cup to the continent of Europe rather than confine the match to Great Britain and Ireland. The older generation of golfers threw up their hands in horror and indignation, but time has proved the wisdom of the move.

Brian Huggett MBE, who played in six Ryder Cups and captained the side once, argues that the inclusion of the rest of Europe was correct because only 50% of the British and Irish players were genuinely good enough to take part. He says: 'You can't expect to beat the Americans with half a team.'

Huggett's boyhood hero and fellow Welshman, Dai Rees, guided Britain to a rare triumph at Lindrick in Sheffield in 1957 but it was an isolated success. Twenty-four years had elapsed since the home nation's last win, and another 28 years would pass before Europe began to redress the balance.

In between times, Britain produced many fine professionals who might have benefited from the inclusion of the rest of Europe. It seems almost inconceivable that players of the calibre of Huggett, Jacklin, Neil Coles, Bernard Gallacher, Peter Oosterhuis and Brian Barnes never savoured a Ryder Cup victory.

Many, however, had their moments. Barnes is unlikely ever to forget the 1975 match with the United States at Laurel Valley, Pennsylvania, where he had the temerity to beat Nicklaus 4 and 2 in the morning singles on the last day.

The great man's pride was injured, and when the pair were drawn together in the afternoon, vengeance seemed inevitable. Barnes, one of the most phlegmatic characters to tramp Britain's fairways, simply clamped his pipe more firmly between his teeth and won 2 and 1. Since that day he has been identified as 'the man who beat Jack Nicklaus twice in a day'.

During the seventies, the Americans were winning by ridiculously wide margins and Nicklaus himself admitted: 'Something has to be done to make it more of a match for the Americans.'

At first, the European influence did not produce the desired effect, even with Seve Ballesteros in 1979 and Bernhard Langer in '81. Then Jacklin was offered the captaincy — despite being omitted from the last-named match at Walton Heath.

'Only if we do things first class,' demanded Jacklin. The P.G.A. readily agreed and the 1983 side flew to Florida on Concorde. The European challenge was off and running, or rather flying.

That year, the United States won by a solitary point. Relief was etched on the face of their captain, Nicklaus, who feared he might become the first American to surrender the Ryder Cup on that side of the ocean. Time would ensure that his anxiety became a reality four years later.

By now it was clear that European golfers were catching up quickly in terms of ability . . . and several had valid reasons for wanting to deflate American egos.

Ballesteros believed he had been mistreated by the U.S.P.G.A. during his early forays outside Europe; Jacklin wanted to win to exorcise the 'years of frustration, rejection and loneliness' in the United States; Sandy Lyle says simply: 'I just love knocking hell out of the Americans on their own soil!'

Several theories have been advanced on the reasons for British golf's resurgence during the eighties. Ryder Cup player Peter Oosterhuis, now domiciled in America, can hazard a guess from his base in New Jersey. 'There is obviously a massive difference in the performances of the European players in the 15 years since I was full-time on that circuit. Maybe it's because there is so much money in the States. Players probably accept finishing in the top more easily than they used to instead of striving to win.

INTRODUCTION

'You can make $500,000 or $600,000 a year in America without ever winning. Those players don't discover what it takes to win, unlike the British and European players. I also feel the courses in Europe demand more variety in shot making, and then there is Seve. Every player on the European tour is aiming at him. And if they can compete with Ballesteros, they feel they can cope with any golfer coming out of America.'

Certainly, there was no sign of an inferiority complex when Jacklin captained the European team for the first time on home soil in 1985. Few will forget the uplifting moment when Sam Torrance clinched the Ryder Cup at the Belfry, caressing his birdie putt against Andy North into the hole at the 18th.

'It was pure theatre,' beamed Jacklin, who led a posse of golfers, officials, wives and well-wishers onto that green to hug Torrance, who stood motionless with both arms raised in a clenched fist salute, tears streaming down his face.

Two years later, Europe finally achieved the breakthrough on American soil. Nicklaus's worst fears were realised, and the irony was greater for the fact that Jacklin's side won at Muirfield Village (The Golden Bear's own creation) in Ohio (his home town).

Jacklin could almost qualify for two chapters in this book: one to document his exceptional golfing exploits and the other to record his feats as a truly outstanding Ryder Cup captain. But in the opinion of this observer, the other 10 golfers also merit their inclusion for a variety of reasons. Most have won major championships, although others like Dai Rees, Eric Brown, Christy O'Connor, Bernard Gallacher and (to date) Ian Woosnam have not.

However, Rees displayed wonderful leadership qualities in captaining the Ryder Cup team a record five times. Brown remains the only person to have won all his single matches in that highly competitive event.

By contrast, Max Faulkner, the 1951 Open champion, could not win any of his Ryder Cup singles. Gallacher simply revelled in the gladiatorial arena of high-pressure match-play.

The final choice is unlikely to meet with universal approval, but if beauty is in the eye of the beholder, so picking 11 golfing greats is also a matter of personal taste.

As long as golf exists, there will also be humour. When Sandy Lyle celebrated his 31st birthday, Bernard Gallacher threw a surprise party for his fellow Scot and Wentworth neighbour.

Gallacher also invited along Lyle's old foe — and another of the 'Wentworth set' — Nick Faldo. The night went with a swing and as the partygoers enjoyed themselves, Gallacher handed Lyle a birthday present.

Sandy undid the wrapping and pulled out a video entitled 'Play Good Golf' . . . by Nick Faldo.

1
HENRY COTTON

THERE is surely no better place to begin a book on Golfing Greats than with the greatest.

It may be inadvisable to attempt to judge one generation against another, but in this instance the evidence points to the inescapable conclusion: Henry Cotton was the best of them all.

'Maestro' is a word to be used sparingly, but it was widely applied to Sir Thomas Henry Cotton MBE, and with ample justification.

Fred Daly, Max Faulkner, Tony Jacklin, Sandy Lyle and Nick Faldo would figure on any post-war shortlist, but the lobby for Cotton is the most persuasive.

Irishman Daly, four years younger than Cotton and relieved of the Open Championship trophy by the old master in 1948, has no reservations. Nor does the respected golfer, author and broadcaster Peter Alliss.

'Henry would have been out on his own today. He was the best, no question of doubt about it,' insisted Fred, who was fortunate enough to study Cotton's career at close quarters for many years.

Alliss, in his book *Supreme Champions of Golf*, was equally decisive in his appraisal of Cotton. He wrote: 'For me, he is not only the greatest British player of the last 60 years but also the best ever. In his own way he has been one of the most caring and influential contributors to British golf this century.'

Few golfers have commanded such a blend of reverence and adoration as the former public schoolboy who drove himself to unreasonable limits in order to become a champion and who pioneered a new era of respectability for professional golf.

Cotton's contribution to British golf cannot be underrated. As he rose to prominence in the decade before the War, so did the status of the humble, often downtrodden professional.

In the words of Fred Daly, Cotton was 'a gentleman'. He also oozed charm, elegance, style, wit and sophistication . . . a formidable armoury which carried considerable clout at some of the more elitist clubs.

Professionals had been regarded as necessary evils in some establishments, good only for mending clubs, tending greens and lending their expertise on the practice ground at ridiculously low rates of pay.

Daly readily admits the debt he and his contemporaries owe Cotton, who used his influence and breeding to break down those class barriers. 'Henry was the one who got us into golf clubs,' explained Fred. 'I mean, being a pro in those days before the War meant there were a whole lot of clubs we weren't allowed into. Henry was the kind of fella who opened all those kinds of doors for us.

'It helped greatly that he was such an educated man, as well as being a wonderful fella. As a matter of fact, if it hadn't been for him, none of us would be where we are today. He made professional golf what it is.'

Cotton's contribution to British golf in general was immense, but he was also phenomenally successful as a player, capturing three Open Championships in 1934, '37 and '48 before opting out of the rigorous routine of top-level competition.

In order to reach the upper echelons he became a slave to golf, and despite damaging his health in pursuit of his goals, never for a moment regretted any of it.

Cotton was rebellious, arrogant and self-opinionated, which is just as well, otherwise the sport might have lost one of its finest ambassadors to cricket. The story of how Henry came to play the Royal and Ancient game epitomises the single-mindedness of the man.

Henry was born in Holmes Chapel, Cheshire, in January, 1907, but after the Cotton family moved south to Dulwich his father sent Henry and elder brother Leslie to Alleyn's public school for a proper middle-class education.

Cricket was Henry's passion at the time and both he and brother Leslie won their colours at that sport with golf figuring only haphazardly in the Cotton curriculum.

He later recalled the episode which was to change his life. 'In those days I was a better cricketer than a golfer. I was the Under-14 captain and made my way into the first eleven as a good first wicket bat.

'Leslie left school to become a professional golfer, but I was lucky in being a bit better academically and I wanted to stay on at school with a view to perhaps going to university and then, perhaps, on to a career in civil engineering.'

However, that pipedream changed radically when the cricket team went to Marlow and the match ended early. Cotton was one of four boys ordered to heave the cricket kit back to Dulwich, and took umbrage at being forced to undertake such a menial chore while the prefects avoided the hard labour. The apparent injustice prompted Henry to lead a revolt of the four non-prefects in the team, who wrote a letter of protest to the games master at Alleyn's. Instead of sympathy, the 'mutineers' were told to submit to a caning by the prefects.

'I refused to be caned,' said Henry many years later. 'So I was banned from cricket until I submitted to the caning. I can still remember my answer to the headmaster when he asked me what I would do when the rest of the boys were playing cricket. I said: "I'll play golf, sir!" '

And play golf he did, to such a level of excellence that it scarcely bears thinking about that Cotton might have complied with the public humiliation of a caning. Who knows? The name of Henry Cotton might even now be sitting alongside that of W.G. Grace as one of the all-time greats in that sporting sphere!

Be it golf or cricket, Cotton was destined to be a champion. His above-average intellect allowed him to discipline himself to the long hours of pain and sacrifice involved in reaching the top, while all the time the flame of desire burned within him.

His father, a 16 handicapper, encouraged Henry and Leslie to take up golf, and by the age of 11 or 12 the younger son decided he was ready for a tilt at the 'old man' off scratch. 'I managed to persuade him to let me play him off level,' said Henry. 'I beat him and he recalled later my telling him: "Father, you will never beat me again". He never did.'

Cotton turned professional at 16, obtaining the appointment as a junior assistant at Fulwell and committing himself wholeheartedly to the task of becoming a worldbeater. The two young Cotton brothers rigged up a net in the garage beside their house and spent endless hours pounding thousands of balls into it in search of a grooved swing.

The exercises were successful in building up his golfing muscles, but the constant repetition of the swing pattern, plus many hours in a bent back position for putting practice, left Henry with deformation of his spine.

He developed back cramps and a permanent list because of the time spent locked in the same position on the practice ground. But his dedication also cultivated an immensely strong pair of wrists, which Cotton believed he required to add length to accuracy.

Henry hit on one idea, which was to wade into knee-length grass and swish away furiously with a club to build up his strength. He remarked once: 'When I was building my career I practised until dark, often by lamplight, concentrating on every shot and every putt was to win the Open.

'I had the desire to be Open champion and I did everything within my power to achieve that goal. I realised I wasn't going to be a physical giant but I made myself stronger. If I had been stronger still, I would have been even better.

'I realised early on that golf was played from the elbows down and all the rest was flavouring. I built my hands and my arms up until I had them very strong to the point where I could hit the ball with my left hand and right hand independently and almost as well as with both together.'

Henry also believed that a full pivot was important in the mechanics of the golf swing and devised a method to remind himself of that. Before gripping the club he usually pulled the glove firmly onto his left hand, and there written in bold print on the palm of the glove was the legend: 'Turn, you idiot!' It worked.

Once Cotton had set out on his pursuit of excellence, things moved quickly. He left Fulwell after nine months and moved to Rye before taking up an appointment as full professional at Langley Park, Beckenham, in 1926 at the age of 19.

The following summer he played in the Open Championship at St. Andrews and finished a creditable eighth behind the incomparable Bobby Jones. Cotton's voracious hunger for knowledge led him to ask the question: Why was it that American golfers appeared to be better than British?

There was only one way to find out. He scraped together £300, partly from his earnings as runner-up in the *News of the World* Match-Play, and booked himself a passage to the United States — first class of course — in November 1928.

The visit enabled Cotton to complete his golfing apprenticeship. Tommy Armour and Sam Snead dispensed advice willingly. Henry listened, learned, and absorbed the different methods and techniques.

He soon discovered he was shorter off the tee than the Americans, and Armour persuaded him to switch from a fade to a draw to obtain extra length. The move was a success and Cotton returned to Britain richer in experience and a few dollars better off following a third-place finish in the Sacramento Open.

Cotton's improvement could be seen in 1929 when he made his Ryder Cup debut at Moortown, beating the highly-rated Al Watrous 4 and 3 to play his part in a British victory.

It was to be his last Ryder Cup appearance for eight years. He warred regularly with his fellow professionals, who saw him as conceited and arrogant rather than visionary. His penchant for Savile Row monogrammed shirts also did little to endear him to the establishment.

That antagonism and jealousy led to his exclusion from the Ryder Cup teams until 1937, but persuaded him to make an important career decision. If his fellow Brits were happy to be regarded as inferior, so be it. But Henry believed the profession was being treated shabbily.

The fact that caddies were paid almost as much for carrying clubs as the players were for playing and teaching offended Cotton's view of fair play. 'I thought I was worth more than that,' he said candidly. And soon after, he took up the offer to become professional at the Royal Waterloo club near Brussels, despite criticism that he was walking out on his country.

Cotton recalled: 'I never regretted the decision and I believe that I did the right thing. It seemed to me that visiting players to Britain received better treatment than the home-based ones.'

From his base on the other side of the English Channel, Cotton began to acquire the respectability he sought and also started to enjoy the fruits of his labour. In consecutive years he led after the first, second and third rounds of the Open Championship. On the last occasion at St. Andrews in 1933 he finished in a tie for seventh place, only three strokes behind Densmore Shute and Craig Wood. At last Henry Cotton was ready to win an Open . . . or was he?

When Cotton arrived at Sandwich for the 1934 championship at Royal St. George's he brought with him four sets of golf clubs and seemed incapable of making much impression with any of them.

However, Henry had come to play so he decided he might as well give it a whirl. A few days later, he played so majestically that he gave a name to a golf ball, the Dunlop 65, which is still being bashed round courses today. Long after the '34 Open, Henry still had the Dunlop ball (a number six) which served him proud that day.

Cotton qualified easily thanks to a first-round 66 and opened up the championship proper with a 67, by courtesy of an outward 31. Henry was in the lead by three strokes.

His second-round 65, which motivated Dunlop to give their product a new name, is generally regarded as one of the great championship performances. It gave him a two-round aggregate of 132 — still a record for any of the four major championships.

That single-round record stood for 43 years, until American Mark Hayes reduced Turnberry to 63 blows in 1977. It meant a nine-stroke lead for Cotton going into the last day.

Cotton's concentration was such that he remembered little of that remarkable round, with the exception of a shot he later described as 'possibly one of the greatest ever played'.

He was already three under fours when he pushed a No 2 iron into a near-impossible lie in a bunker at the par-three eighth. He recalled: 'I knew I was in terrible trouble.

'The ball was plugged in the sand and the big danger in trying to play it was that if the shot didn't come off the ball would trickle down into the huge footprints I had made, from where it would be totally unplayable.

'I considered taking a drop under penalty but I decided in the end to play the ball as it lay. The shot came off. I got the ball to within six yards of the pin and I think that was the most remarkable shot I can recall playing. In fact I think it may have been one of the greatest shots ever played and very few people actually saw it.'

Cotton added: 'Not only was it one of the most important moments in my career, it was probably the toughest shot I ever played, particularly in the circumstances in which I played it.'

From that moment Henry sailed on serenely towards his 65, which was followed by a 72 on the last morning. He now enjoyed the luxury of a 10-stroke advantage, and the probability of the first British winner for 10 years brought the crowds flocking to the south coast.

The last afternoon almost went horribly wrong. For some years, Cotton had suffered from ill-health. Apart from a twisted spine caused by the long hours of practice, he developed gastric problems due to an incorrect diet and the stresses of playing high-pressure tournament golf. A specialist diagnosed stomach ulcers and that suspect constitution resulted in Cotton being invalided out of the R.A.F. during the Second World War.

On that particular day at Sandwich it was rumoured that something had disagreed with Cotton at lunch, but a more likely reason is that the tension involved in the Open induced a severe attack of stomach cramps.

Henry scrambled to the turn in 40, with a pair of sixes on his card, before starting back with three straight fives. All that and some of the toughest holes ahead of him. It seemed that the most spectacular collapse in golfing history was going to rob Cotton of the coveted title.

However, a delicate pitch and putt of 12 feet earned Cotton a four at the 13th and that broke the spell. The Maestro's nerves vanished along with the stomach cramps and he finished with a clutch of par figures for an ugly but effective 79. That moderate round still managed to secure the trophy by five strokes with a record-equalling score of 283.

It was the vital breakthrough 27-year-old Cotton needed, and his second victory at Carnoustie in 1937 suggests that the intervention of the War deprived him of further triumphs during those prime years of his life. The demanding Scottish links, once described by American Hale Irwin as a 'sleeping giant', was wide awake on this occasion and a cruel test at 7200 yards from the back tees.

However, the Americans had just won the Ryder Cup on British soil for the first time, and with Sam Snead, Byron Nelson, Walter Hagen and Gene Sarazen in the Open field, it seemed a matter of which Yank collected the title.

In qualifying, the Americans were outstanding, but as the weather deteriorated, many of the overseas players saw their hopes washed away.

Cotton was four strokes adrift at halfway but in the foulest weather closed on the leaders with a third-round 73. After the agonies of Sandwich, it suited Henry to creep up quietly from behind this time.

His closing 71 stands comparison with his 65 at St. George's. The rain came slanting down and the sodden course was virtually waterlogged as Cotton squelched his way to victory.

He covered the first six holes of the last round in two under par, helped by five chips and single putts. Henry reached the last knowing he could afford a six and still pick up his second title. Avoiding the out of bounds skirting the left-hand side of the fairway, Cotton took a five for a total of 290 and a two-shot win over Reg Whitcombe.

Twelve months later Whitcombe finally captured an Open at Sandwich, scene of Cotton's record-breaking 1934 triumph. This time gale-force winds disrupted the event and Henry surged through the field on the final afternoon to finish third, his 74 being the best score in conditions when only seven of the 36 starters broke 80.

It was one of Cotton's abiding regrets that he was forced to abandon competitive golf to accommodate Herr Hitler. 'I wouldn't have minded missing a couple of wars,' he once confided. 'I would like to think I would have won a couple more Opens, but that's life.'

There was to be one more Open success at Muirfield in 1948, but prior to that Cotton served his time in the R.A.F. until his fragile constitution and a burst appendix forced him out of military service.

However, before failing to meet the medical requirements, he nevertheless made a valuable contribution to the War effort through his golf. Max Faulkner, an old friend and frequent adversary, remembered one particular incident. 'I was training Royal Marines at

Whitley Bay and Henry was stationed not far away. He found out I was there and immediately organised an exhibition match for the Red Cross.

'On the last, Henry called out to the big crowd following us: "Would you please donate ten shillings . . . but wrap them around half crowns to prevent the notes from blowing away!" He was a crafty one, but we made a heck of a lot of money for a good cause.' Cotton, in fact, devoted so much time to that organisation that his sterling work for the Red Cross was recognised by his being awarded the MBE at the end of the War.

After hostilities ceased, Henry figured prominently in the 1946 and '47 Opens before his weakened condition told against him. Visits to Monte Carlo and America cured that problem and Cotton was a happy and well-fortified man when he arrived at Muirfield in 1948. The fairways were no more than narrow avenues between acres of deep rough and he revelled in the conditions, claiming to have hit 52 out of 56 fairways.

An opening 70 was an acceptable start, but inspiration was at hand when Henry was introduced to King George VI before the start of his second round. Cotton shook the regal hand and launched a drive and three wood on to the green. A birdie putt followed and Cotton was on his way to demoralising the field with a record 66.

Fred Daly, the 1947 champion, still shakes his head in recollection of that round. 'If it hadn't been for that inspired round I would have retained the title,' he said sadly.

'Of course it was disappointing for me personally, but that doesn't detract from the fact that it was a remarkable round of golf. The rest of us never had a chance after that.'

Cotton closed with rounds of 75 and 72, and could afford another last-round slip at the 18th, where he took two to escape from a bunker and finished with a bogey five — yet still won in a canter by five strokes from Daly.

By now Cotton was 41 years of age and that third Open triumph persuaded him to begin winding down on his tournament appearances to concentrate on other aspects of his varied career.

He became a journalist and author and dabbled in golf course architecture, creating a masterpiece in Penina on the Portuguese Algarve.

Meanwhile he never lost his zest for teaching the game . . . especially after he hit upon the novel idea of using a rubber tyre as a means of strengthening the arms and wrists. Many a pupil graduated through the Cotton academy after learning the secrets of the tyre method.

Before quitting competitive golf altogether he finished fourth in the 1952 Open at Hoylake, and was still knocking it round at Turnberry in 1977 at the age of 70 — purely in the interest of nostalgia. It was a weary Cotton who shot 93 and admitted: 'I've never had a 93 in my life. I hope no-one is ashamed of me.'

In 1949 he played in his sixth *News of the World* Match-Play final, losing to Dai Rees to complete his association with that tournament with three wins and three second-place finishes to his name.

The Ryder Cup also figured prominently in Cotton's career again during the forties and fifties, when he captained the British and Irish team on two occasions.

Unfortunately, the 1947 clash in Portland, Oregon, was an unmitigated disaster as Cotton's side were hammered 11-1 by a powerful American team. Despite that defeat, one of the 'victims', Max Faulkner, can still see the funny side of that match.

'I will always remember Henry as a wonderful player, a good Ryder Cup captain, and a very temperamental chap. When he wanted things done, they were done. The night before the match in Portland we were all summoned to his room for — we thought — a team talk.

'Instead Henry insisted we all get down on our knees and say a prayer. Some of the players, myself included, thought it was a bit strange but no-one argued. Henry asked the Lord to help us the next day but he obviously wasn't listening!'

That match was Cotton's last as a player, but he was awarded the non-playing captaincy six years later at Wentworth, where the finger of blame for a narrow home defeat was pointed at him.

Henry decided to play two inexperienced men, Peter Alliss and Bernard Hunt, near the bottom of the order in the singles. Both played the last indifferently and America won by a single point.

However, the biggest headlines were reserved for Mrs Cotton, as fiercely protective a wife as any man could have. Henry had met 'Toots', a wealthy Argentinian heiress, at the Mar del Plata club in January 1930 and together they forged a formidable partnership.

In 1953, the Americans led 3-1 after the first day at Wentworth and Cotton told reporters he had 'kicked his players around the dressing room'. He hadn't meant it literally, but the following morning the newspaper billboards carried banner headlines declaring that the captain was ashamed of his team. Toots' Latin temperament got the better of her and she proceeded to rip down the placards from the roads leading into Wentworth declaring: 'All the papers have told lies about Henry!'

Cotton was a truly international golfer in an era notable for its insularity. He was never afraid to travel in order to play golf and won a clutch of tournaments on the Continent as well as one each in North and South America.

He was also a showman, an entertainer . . . and not just on the golf course. In 1938 a theatrical agent coaxed Henry into appearing at the London Coliseum. Toots and Henry got to work perfecting an act suitable to top the bill, hitting on the idea of treating his bag, shoes, clubs and golf balls in a phosphorescent paint which glowed brightly in the dark. Much to Cotton's surprise, his variety performance was a big hit and many more shows followed.

As the years rolled by, Cotton spent more time writing on wide-ranging golf topics, acting in an advisory capacity for BBC Television's commentary team at major events, and devoting himself to turning Penina into a heaven on earth.

In that, he succeeded and both Toots, who died on Christmas Day in 1982, and Henry are buried close to his magnificent creation. Shortly before his death in December

1987, Cotton learned that he was to be knighted; an honour which many close associates felt should have been bestowed on him years earlier.

Cotton once wrote that golf was 'more than a game to me; it is a life's work'. That life was lived to the full and gave immense pleasure to many people. It will always be argued whether he truly was the greatest, but in the final analysis it doesn't matter. He was simply The Maestro.

CAREER RECORD
MAJOR TITLES: British Open 1934-37-48.
OVERSEAS TITLES: Belgian Open 1930-34-38; Mar Del Plata Open (Argentina) 1930; Italian Open 1936; German Open 1937-38-39; Czechoslovakian Open 1937-38; French Open 1946-47; White Sulphur Springs Invitation (U.S.A.) 1948.
DOMESTIC TITLES: Dunlop Southport Tournament 1931-32; P.G.A. Match-Play 1932-40-46; *Yorkshire Evening News* Tournament 1935-47; Dunlop Metropolitan Tournament 1936; Silver King Tournament 1937; *Daily Mail* Tournament 1939; *News Chronicle* Tournament 1945; *Star* Tournament 1946; Spalding Tournament 1947; Dunlop Tournament 1953; Penfold Tournament 1954.
INTERNATIONAL: Ryder Cup 1929-37-47; GB v France 1929.
MISC: P.G.A. captain 1934-48; Vardon Trophy (Order of Merit) 1938; Tooting Bec Cup (Lowest round by GB and I resident in Open) 1947 (jt)-48; Ryder Cup captain 1947-53; knighted 1987.

2
FRED DALY

E VEN the greatest names in world golf regularly acknowledge that they wouldn't be
where they are today without the counselling of some wise old guru. Few, however,
feel they owe a debt of gratitude to their tailor.

While others have spent years in the vain pursuit of perfection on the practice
ground, Fred Daly cried 'Eureka' when searching not for a new swing but a new jacket!

For years, the man who was destined to become the first, and so far only, Irishman to
lay his hands on the Open Championship trophy had been puzzled about an inclination to
hook the ball off the tee. There was no obvious answer to the problem, but he recognised it
was interfering with his progress towards golf's upper echelons.

As often happens, the secret was ridiculously simple. The year was 1938 and
Fred explained: 'I never could cope with a deep-faced club like a driver. I tended to hit
the ball with a high hook so I changed to a No 2 wood and sacrificed some length to keep
it straight.

'It was successful up to a point but accuracy alone is not enough if you want to reach
the very top in professional golf. I needed the extra yardage and tried without any luck to
find a solution.

'Then one day I went along to be measured for a new jacket and my tailor remarked
that I was short in the arms and he would need to cut some material off the cuffs. Suddenly
I hit upon the idea of using a longer club.'

Like an inventor hot on the trail of a major discovery, Fred worked feverishly to find
out if his theory had a practical application. He selected a bulky Gene Sarazen model
driver and set about modifying it.

'I took off the grip and burned the "plug" out of the shaft and made my own.
By lunchtime, the club was about six inches longer. It felt good, but was now a bit too
long, so I cut it down until it was two inches longer than average.

'I put the leather grip back onto the driver and headed straight for the first hole at
Lurgan, which was about 290 yards or so, all carry. I hit the first two or three shots all right
but they were going in different directions.

'Then, at about the fifth attempt, I cracked this tremendous shot clean onto the middle of the green . . . and that's how I learned about the effectiveness of the longer shaft. I was off and running.'

It proved to be a turning point in Daly's career. From that moment he always used a 44 inch long driver and had his irons specially adapted to increase their length by about one and a half inches. Fred chuckled: 'I was noted for hitting the ball long and straight, but few people knew how I found the secret.'

After years of fighting a hook, Fred now felt that the driver was tailor-made for him, as it were. And it was the driver — although not that particular model — which held the key to his Open Championship triumph at the Royal Liverpool club in Hoylake in 1947. But more of that story later.

Fred Daly came into the world in that golfers' paradise of Portrush on the most northerly tip of Ulster in October, 1911, the youngest of six children. Within no time, the youngster was lured by the magnetic qualities of the vast, rolling links.

'I was born about an eight iron from the course, so I developed a "feel" for the game right away. My father and brothers were artisan members but the most important influences on my career were the really good local players.

'Luckily, we had some great golfers at Portrush in those days and as a caddie boy from about the age of nine I was able to learn little bits and pieces from each of them.

'Once you graduated to the rank of first-class caddie, you got the best players to work for. I never had an official lesson in my life but I used to look, listen and learn in those early days.'

Fred soon picked up the rudiments of the game and the first person to fully appreciate his obsession for golf was his schoolteacher . . . when she discovered a grubby little club behind the classroom door!

'I took that club everywhere,' laughed Fred. 'We were seldom parted. I remember it started life as a carpet beater which an old lady gave me. However, I took it down to the golf course and battered it into the shape of an iron.'

Daly left school at the traditional age of 14 and commenced his golfing education by trudging round Portrush twice a day as a caddie and a third time playing with his basic set of three clubs.

At the age of 16 or 17 he began his apprenticeship as an electrician, a career which lasted only a few months. An important amateur event was due to be played at Portrush and Fred wanted to caddie. He was refused permission to take time off — so the electrical trade had one less employee from that moment.

'I couldn't resist the golf. I had to go and caddie even if it meant I was finished as an electrician. But it paid off in the end because a gentleman whose bag I carried regularly got me a summer professional's job at Mahee Island, a nine-hole course in County Down. I was 20 and I've been on the road ever since.'

During the winters Fred signed on the 'dole' for 25 shillings a week and stayed fit by playing a round of golf every day and involving himself in other sports such as badminton and hockey.

Life, as Fred readily admits, was tough in those years between the two World Wars. Under the rules of the day, he had to serve a three-year apprenticeship at a club before earning a penny from tournaments. Nowadays, any Tom, Dick or Seve can join the circuit without that basic grounding.

'It doesn't seem to matter whether you can fit a grip or not. The requirements are so different now. At Mahee Island I had to carry out all the jobs — professional, greenkeeper, steward, everything — while my wife, Jean, was left with the cooking.'

Looking back on those times, Daly was forced to admit he envied many of the current breed of tournament professionals, whose only concern is to negotiate their way around a particular golf course.

'I would love to have had a manager, like these pros today. I honestly believe I could have done better if someone had taken me under their wing. When I was a young man you had to take care of everything yourself; buy a ticket to England or Scotland, organise transport at the other end and find suitable accommodation.

'You went to the docks in Belfast to grab a boat on a Monday night and you were off. Usually, you didn't even know if you would get a berth. The tournament started on Wednesday, finished on Friday — if you qualified — and then it was a mad dash back to Ireland to be at your club on Saturday morning.

'These fellas nowadays disappear in April and don't come back for about five months! It's a world of a difference. Today's players don't have any distractions. They just get on a plane knowing that everything has been taken care of. That was part of the reason I never tried my luck in America. I had no-one like Mark McCormack to help me.'

However, back in the thirties and early forties, it was a case of the Americans coming to Daly rather than the other way around.

After completing his apprenticeship, Fred's tournament career began promisingly when he won the Ulster Championship in 1935 — the first of a record 13 victories. He had also taken the advice of a leading player, Willie Nolan, to abandon a two-fisted grip and switch to the Vardon method.

In the spring of 1939 he moved to the City of Derry club for £3 10 shillings a week. Then came the War, and Fred's plans to plunder the tournaments in England and Scotland were shelved for six years.

It was a difficult time to eke out a living . . . until the American troops started arriving at Lough Foyle. 'I worked hard teaching the Yanks. The American Government had allowed so many sets of clubs to be brought over — about six or seven clubs in a small white bag — and there was no shortage of business.

'The biggest problem was that no-one was manufacturing golf balls or golf clubs during the War years. We had to make do with clubs which were lying around the shop and you had to go out and find the balls.

'There is no doubt that the War set me back a long way, in terms of my tournament career. I missed out on the prime years of my life, but there was some compensation. I applied for the job at Balmoral in Belfast in March, 1944 and was hired for £5 a week — the highest salary of any club professional in Ireland at the time.

'I'm pleased to say I am still there all these years later,' added Fred proudly. 'Fortunately they didn't try to pension me off when I reached the age of 65 and I will always be grateful to the club for their support over the years.'

Daly was already 33 years old when he embarked on his first foray across the Irish Sea to play in the *Daily Mail* Victory Tournament at St. Andrews towards the end of 1945. But the experience wasn't wasted on him. For the first time in his life, he realised he was as good as, if not better than, the majority of the field.

'Considering it was my first time out of Ireland, I was pleased to tie for third place. I took a nine at the long 14th in the last round and finished with three fives but still shared third spot.

'I remember winning £81 and going back home and handing Jean £41 to put aside for the following season. I told her: "If that's the best those fellows can do, I can make my way among them".

'It was an especially good performance because I didn't like the Old Course at St. Andrews. Never have done. There were so many bunkers I always maintained that someone went out during the night and made new ones!

'There were too many unfair bumps and borrows as well. At Portrush you got the reward for a good shot but at St. Andrews you could hit a fine approach to the stick and find it nowhere near the hole.

'All those things got me thinking about the standard required. If I could finish third, in my first tournament across the water, on a course I didn't like, with such a ridiculous score for the last few holes, what could I do when all the conditions were right?'

The next two years would provide a triumphant answer to those questions. If that brief flirt with British tournament golf whetted Daly's appetite for more, 1946 made him positively ravenous.

It was the season which established him as Ireland's top player by some considerable distance, and re-affirmed his own impression that he could compete on an equal footing with men of the calibre of Cotton, Rees and Faulkner.

That year, Fred won a seventh Ulster Championship, finished joint eighth behind Sam Snead in his first Open Championship (back at unfavoured St. Andrews), collected the Irish Closed Championship, reached the quarter-finals of the *News of the World* Match-Play and took fourth place in the Dunlop Masters at Stoneham. But most important of all, he became the first Irishman to capture the Irish Open.

The tournament was in its 19th year and all Ireland had been yearning for someone to hero-worship. Little Fred Daly, all five foot six of him, was happy to oblige at Portmarnock.

'That was a significant win. It was a big thrill to be the first Irish golfer to achieve a home victory and my career really took off from that moment,' confessed Fred.

After two rounds, Daly was on 145, just a stroke behind Bobby Locke, but confident that the breaks would come. Sure enough, they did in a third round which enabled him to more than double his winnings for the week.

'The winner's cheque was £150, but the Portmarnock members had offered another £200 to anyone breaking 70 that week,' recalled Fred. 'They probably didn't believe it could be done but I believed that I could collect.

'I went to the turn in 32 then struggled a bit on the way home and needed a par on the last for my 69. I got it, which was a relief, although I felt I should have scored 67.

'The reaction of the crowd was incredible. I was chaired all the way from the last green to the clubhouse, even although I had another round to play. They were more excited than I was!

'Fortunately nothing could distract me on the golf course. Even if I was feeling unwell, or a bit "strung up" before a round, all the problems disappeared as soon as I hit the first tee shot. Everything else went out of my mind.'

With Locke carding a 72, Daly was the leader by two strokes. Suddenly a thunderstorm came in off the sea and dampened the South African's enthusiasm. Locke's closing 76 was beaten by Daly's 74 — and the Irish could finally claim a champion of their own.

And so to Hoylake. Exactly nine years after he had stumbled across the 'short arms, long driver' theory, he kept an appointment with destiny at the Royal Liverpool club. The course was set up in such a way that the Open was begging to be won by a long, accurate, driver. Fred fitted the bill exactly.

'You know, at the start of the 1947 season I had no thoughts about winning the Open. None whatsoever,' he maintained. 'The only time it entered the conversation was a few weeks before I left for Hoylake.

'I was playing with a fellow professional at home in Ireland and he turned to me and said: "I've never seen anyone hit the ball as well as you, Fred. I'm going to back you for the Open". So it turned out that a lot of people put their money where their mouths were at the rewarding odds of 33-1.'

Anyway, when Fred eventually arrived at Hoylake, the course met all his criteria. 'It was the ideal driver's course, demanding accuracy and length off the tee. To make things even better, the greens were hard and fast, just the way I liked them.

'We played one round at Hoylake and the local pro, Cyril Hughes, asked to join us. That gave us a valuable insight to any hidden dangers before I decided to play at the nearby Arrowe Park course. We called it Narrow Park because of the tight fairways, and that confirmed what I already knew . . . my game was in good shape for the Open.'

Daly qualified comfortably on 145, then sprinted into a commanding four-stroke lead at halfway following rounds of 73 and 70. Henry Cotton and Sam King from Wildernesse were his nearest pursuers.

Suddenly the master plan threatened to fall apart. On the final morning Fred compiled halves of 36 and 42 for a potentially fatal 78. His lead had been wiped out — but at least he wasn't behind as he shared a total of 221 with three others, including Cotton. More to the point, his indomitable spirit had not been broken.

'I felt absolutely terrible after that 78. I knew I had played well but I committed the crime of getting "cagey" and trying to protect my lead. That round was a valuable lesson as it taught me never to be defensive. Instead of attacking and going for birdies and maybe getting pars, I was thinking about making par and getting bogies! It went against my natural inclinations.

'It would have been easy to let that 78 get to me but I felt I simply hadn't got any breaks so I wasn't too concerned. At lunch I told myself: "This is it . . . go for everything. No going sideways. Look for the pin and aim at it".'

True to his word, Daly launched into the final round with a brand of uninhibited, swashbuckling golf. His closing 72 was not without flaws, but it was certainly effective.

He reached the turn in 38, covered the next five holes in two over threes, slipped to a double-bogey six at the 17th and finished flamboyantly with a birdie 3 for an inward 34.

'I took two chips and three putts on the double-tier 17th green and wondered if I had blown it. On the 18th tee I felt like belting the ball into the sea! However, I knew Reg Horne was in the clubhouse on 294 and I needed a birdie to lead the field. And I got it.

'The wind had whipped up so I only needed a drive and No 9 iron, which left me a difficult eight-yard putt across the slope. I mean, from where I was I could have three-putted easily. I picked a spot at the top of the hill and the ball rolled over it . . . and into the hole.'

At that moment Fred knew the title was his, even although dozens of players were still out on the course. His friends, the Whitcombe brothers, dragged him into a quiet corner of the snooker room at Hoylake for a bottle of beer before the news filtered through. Fred Daly was the champion.

'It was funny how it ended,' he said. 'Only Frank Stranahan, the American amateur, could tie if he holed his second shot at the last. People still talk about his attempt and it seems to get closer and closer every time the story is retold. In fact, I'm waiting for a telephone call any day to tell me he's finally holed it and I'm in a play-off! Honestly, I haven't a clue how near he was. I only know that it didn't go in.'

All that remained was for Fred to re-emerge from the snooker room to receive the famous old jug from the Royal Liverpool captain R.J. Hodges and crack a joke: 'The trophy's going to Ireland for the first time. The change of air will do it good!'

Following a wild night of celebration in Liverpool's Adelphi Hotel, Daly and his enthusiastic entourage set sail for Belfast on Saturday night ready to resume the festivities on arrival in Ireland.

'You wouldn't believe it,' said Fred, still groaning at the memory. 'We docked at Belfast and went straight to the Queen's Hotel for a nice breakfast . . . but no drink. It was the day of national prayer, which was always observed very strictly, so alcohol was out.'

Just to prove that Hoylake was not a freak, Fred came agonisingly close to becoming the first golfer since Walter Hagen in 1929 to make a successful defence of the Open title.

In 1948 he was denied only by the supreme excellence of Henry Cotton, whose second-round 66 reduced the Open to a contest for second place. Daly played consistently, shooting 72, 71, 73, 73 to finish five strokes behind Cotton.

'If it hadn't been for Henry I would have retained the title,' he said wistfully. 'That 66 was a tremendous round of golf but I was very unhappy because I felt I was playing well enough to hold on to the championship.

'In fact that Open was doubly disappointing. King George VI attended Muirfield and, as Open champion, I expected to be introduced to him. As it turned out, he met Henry and I was snubbed. I felt badly let down.'

However, that inexplicable oversight was corrected in 1983 when Fred and Jean travelled to Buckingham Palace to attend the investiture ceremony for Fred's MBE. A rendezvous with the Queen was adequate compensation for the snub at Muirfield all those years previously.

Twice more Daly came within striking distance of the Open title, but at Troon in 1950 and Royal Lytham in 1952 he paid the penalty for inconsistency over the four rounds.

After a couple of moderate rounds at Troon, Daly unleashed a 'charge' worthy of Arnold Palmer or Jack Nicklaus, finishing 69, 66 over the gruelling Ayrshire course for a share of third place with Dai Rees, three shots behind Bobby Locke. That closing 66 smashed the course record for Troon and stood for 23 years until the mighty Nicklaus lowered it by a single stroke in the last round of the 1973 championship.

Course records, as it happened, became almost commonplace to Daly during his career. At one stage just after the War he held seven records simultaneously . . . and a few of them still stand to this day.

Two years after that Troon experience Fred produced two imperious rounds of 67 and 69 to lead the field by four strokes. However, Fred, now in his 41st year, failed to sustain that stupendous form and fell away with scores of 77 and 76 to finish third once again.

In between those two close calls, the Open visited Daly's birthplace of Portrush — the only time the great championship has been played outside either England or Scotland. However, the voracious demands of the Irish public and media weighed heavily on their home-grown champion and he was forced to settle for a share of fourth place, a long way behind Max Faulkner.

All this time, the affable Irishman was showing just what an outstanding all-round golfer he was by collecting three *News of the World* Match-Play titles in a six-year spell between 1947 and '52.

During his *annus mirabilis* of 1947, he added the Match-Play to his Open victory, defeating Cotton in the semi-final before going on to beat Flory van Donck of Belgium. A year later, Laurie Ayton became his second victim in the final at Birkdale while the unfortunate van Donck again capitulated at Walton Heath in 1952.

'That win over Cotton was a match which stands out in my mind,' said Fred. 'He was the one we all had to beat and I remember Henry arranging for a large police presence to be on duty on the Saturday, the day of the final. He was confident he would beat me in the semi-final but I won and he was left feeling a bit sheepish!

'In fact, apart from the Open, I would classify my three match-play titles as the highlights of my career. Only Dai Rees won that tournament more times — and of course I did it without using "artificial methods".

'I disagree totally with the policy of measuring every hole, compiling yardage charts and getting information on exact pin positions. That makes it little more than a form of target golf. The game should be played with the eye only, in my opinion.'

With or without yardage charts, few could dispute Daly's uncanny ability to guess distances with the human eye. Certainly not Ted Kroll.

Kroll was an American Ryder Cup golfer who suffered the misfortune of running into Fred Daly in irresistible form during the 1953 clash at Wentworth. It was Fred's fourth successive — and, as it turned out, last — appearance for Britain and Ireland but his 9 and 7 singles win over Kroll is the third biggest victory margin by a British player since Sam Ryder donated his famous trophy in 1927.

'Poor Ted Kroll never knew what hit him. I was in good form that year and in the foursomes, Harry Bradshaw and I had scored Britain's only point in the foursomes the previous day.

'In the singles, I went round Wentworth in 66 strokes during the morning round and there was nothing Kroll could do. I would like to have played in more Ryder Cups, but at least I went out on a high note.

'However, that match wasn't the best I took part in. Funnily enough, it was one I lost. In 1949 at Ganton I faced the former U.S. Open champion Lloyd Mangrum and he shot 65 to my 66 in the first round of the singles.

'I stood one down at lunch but Ben Hogan, the American captain, looked disdainfully at Mangrum and asked: "What happened to you?" Mangrum retorted: "What happened to me? That guy Daly can play, you know. I'm lucky to be one up!" Coming from someone like Mangrum, I took that as a tremendous compliment, even although I did eventually lose on the last green.'

By the mid-fifties, Fred decided it was time to reduce his tournament commitments. He explained: 'I had my job at Balmoral to consider. The members had been patient in putting up with my regular disappearances to play in tournaments but it was time to give them greater consideration.

'In those days it was important to be there at weekends, so as I got older I concentrated on that side of the business. I've been lucky that no pressure was put on me to retire and I'm still officially the head professional there.

'I don't play much these days but if someone comes along with a problem I'll try to sort them out. One thing you never lose is the ability to spot something wrong with the golf swing.'

Balmoral recently named a new lounge in the clubhouse after Fred, and the man himself performed the opening ceremony. 'You can't keep me away from the place,' he chuckled. 'If I'm not there, something must be wrong.'

Even although more than four decades have passed since Daly's Open triumph, he is never short of an audience anxious to hear about that magical moment. The Irish love their sporting heroes . . . and Fred Daly was unquestionably one of the greatest.

CAREER RECORD
MAJOR TITLES: British Open 1947.
DOMESTIC TITLES: Ulster Professional 1936-40-41-42-43-46-51-55-56-57-58; Irish Professional 1940-46-52; Irish Open 1946; Irish Dunlop 1946-52; P.G.A. Match-Play 1947-48-52; Dunlop Southport Tournament 1948; Penfold Tournament 1948; Lotus Tournament 1950; Daks Tournament 1952.
INTERNATIONAL: Ryder Cup 1947-49-51-53; Ireland in World Cup 1954-55.
MISC: Tooting Bec Cup 1950-52; awarded MBE 1983.

3
DAI REES

DAI Rees started life with two distinct advantages. As the son of a professional he was born to golf, while nature saw to it that he was a born golfer as well.

It's one thing to enjoy the privilege of growing up within a gentle sand iron of a golf course, and another altogether to be blessed with God-given talent. David James Rees had both and the combination proved irresistible.

The destinies of most people are shaped gradually over a number of years but Rees knew he was going to be a golfer almost before he could pronounce the word 'fore'.

Dai was not so much born with a silver spoon in his mouth as a cut-down four wood in his hands! And that 'baffie', as it was known, was the club which launched a truly extraordinary career.

World War I was nearly over when his father handed five-year-old Dai that hickory-shafted club along with some worn 'gutty' golf balls.

Not for the first time in his life, Dai showed that being slight of stature was not necessarily a disadvantage in golf. The toddler used a pile of wet sand to tee up his ball at the 300-yard 12th hole at The Leys club where his dad was pro. He smacked three shots down the fairway with his child-size club . . . and proceeded to sink a 60-yard pitch for the first par of his young life.

That single event should have convinced anyone with an interest in Dai's future that he was destined to be a golfer. Two other incidents merely confirmed that belief.

Eunice Rees, who married Dai in 1938 and shared in that marvellous career until his death in November 1983, at the age of 70, recalled the sequence of events which eventually led him to the highest branches of the golfing tree.

'He was brought up in a golf club, encouraged by a father who was a professional, so from the beginning he was steeped in a golfing tradition,' said Mrs Rees. 'However, I recall David — as I knew him — often saying that his mother didn't want him to follow his father into the golf business.

'So for a short period at school he toyed with the idea of being a professional footballer and had trials arranged with Cardiff City. He was quite a good player but on the day of the trial he fell ill with chickenpox, missed the trial, and that effectively ended his footballing ambitions.'

The fact that he surrendered two front teeth after losing an argument with the tarmac during a playground kick-around possibly hastened the decision as well!

But the moment which determined the path Rees would follow came in 1928 when 15-year-old Dai was entered by his father for the Welsh Boys' Championship at Porthcawl.

By this time he had developed a keen interest in the game, and acquired a pencil bag and a set of eight clubs to replace the baffie, mashie and rusty blade putter which had been his constant companions for a number of years. To supplement his pocket money, Dai also earned the odd crust by caddying for club members.

However, Eunice explained what went wrong. She said: 'The powers that be in South Wales at the time returned his entry form for the Boys' Championship, saying that he was earning money from the game. It was so silly because he would only caddie for one or two of the members on a Saturday or Sunday.

'Just because he picked up sixpence or a shilling now and then he was deemed to be a professional. It makes you laugh now to think about the small-minded attitude of the "old school" but it wasn't funny to David at the time.'

However, Rees accepted the rebuff with a philosophical shrug of the shoulders and said: 'All right, if I can't play this game as an amateur I might as well play it as a professional.'

His mind made up, Dai left school immediately and became an assistant to his father at Brynhill and soon after moved to Aberdare where he spent between eight and ten hours every day learning all aspects of professional life.

He was only 15 but 'lived and breathed golf' according to Eunice Rees. That boyish enthusiasm and indefatigable urge to win would never desert him throughout his life and inspired him to contest major tournaments until the early 1970s.

Twice, in his fifties, Rees reached the final of the *News of the World* Match-Play Championship which he won a record four times during the halcyon days, and astounded the younger generation by finishing second in the 1973 Martini International at the ripe old age of 60.

He carved a niche for himself in the Ryder Cup record books by captaining the Great Britain and Ireland side five times, including the famous 1957 victory at Lindrick. That left one glaring omission in the Rees roll of honour . . . the Open Championship.

In the post-war years, few golfers can boast a comparable record of top four finishes in the world's oldest 'major', but fate decreed that the Welsh Wizard failed to conjure up a solitary success.

Three times Dai finished runner-up, twice by a single stroke. On other occasions he was third and fourth — but always the title eluded him. There are no obvious reasons why Rees missed out, although a contemporary, Fred Daly, may have advanced the most plausible theory — that Dai possibly wanted to win too much.

The genial Irishman, whose 1947 Open triumph is detailed elsewhere in this book, insisted: 'Everyone is trying harder to win the title more than any other championship . . . and that's why they don't win it. They try too hard and, frankly, I think Dai was so screwed up inside, so keen to be Open champion, that it prevented him from doing so.

'I remember once at St. Andrews when he knocked his tee shot out of bounds at the first. Now anyone who knows the Old Course will realise it is just about impossible to do that because the fairway is so wide, and someone of Dai's ability should not have done that. But it showed how the Open can affect some people.'

Daly's diagnosis agrees with that of Eunice Rees, who witnessed her husband come so near to achieving his ultimate ambition several times before some calamity overtook him.

'Looking back, maybe he was always a step ahead of himself towards the end of the Opens in which he held a good chance of winning,' she said. 'I suspect he was thinking things like: "I've almost got it" or "This is all I need to do now . . . ". I still wonder if that was the reason.

'In match-play it was one hole at a time and he was a wonderful match-player. He revelled in that form of golf as his tournament record and Ryder Cup performances show.

'But, as I say, he was inclined to look a little too far ahead in stroke-play and maybe it was part of the reason he didn't quite make it. However, he never dwelled on his disappointments, even although he must have felt desperately sad inside.

'I mean, he managed to survive the War after three years in the Middle East, so everything balances out in the end. You count your blessings. In David's case he didn't win an Open but he had his life.'

Before the Second World War, Dai's best placings in the Open were 11th in 1936 and 12th in 1939, but between '46 and '61 he was undeniably the most consistent British or Irish golfer to contest the championship.

In spite of rationing and the general debilitating effects of the War, Rees played himself into a winning position for the first time at St. Andrews in 1946, assisted by a record-breaking 67 in the second round which stood for 14 years.

Going into the final round he was level with Slammin' Sam Snead and one ahead of Henry Cotton but endured the first of several agonising finishes. At the first hole he splashed down in the Swilcan Burn and took a triple bogey seven.

A clutch of five fives followed as the disaster preyed on his mind and the title was blown away with a horrific 80. On leaving the 18th green, his annoyance turned to abject misery when he discovered that a 74 would have been good enough to deprive Snead of the title.

By then it was obvious to Rees, his fellow professionals and the general public that he possessed the necessary shot-making equipment to take the title. At Troon in 1950 he played with commendable consistency, shooting 71, 68, 72, 71 to finish third.

In each round he went to the turn in 33 blows and every time contrived to stumble at the 12th, where he took two bogies and a pair of double-bogies. Six strokes dropped on one hole and Bobby Locke took the title by three.

On paper it might appear that Rees was entirely culpable, and that his own obsessive desire to succeed cost him dearly. However, another little Welsh terrier, Brian Huggett, refuses to accept that was the case. Huggett, cast from the same fiery mould as Rees and raised in the same corner of South Wales, believes that his boyhood hero was simply unlucky.

'As far as I'm concerned, Dai and Christy O'Connor were the two greatest British golfers never to win the Open. They were complete golfers; no failings in technique or temperament, and both came very close,' said Brian.

'Having been second and third myself, I know how it feels to get so near to winning, but I can sleep at nights because I knew I didn't throw it away. I did my best and it wasn't quite good enough and I think the same applied to Dai.

'I don't feel he ever "blew" the Open in the way poor Nicky Price did at Troon in 1982 or Doug Sanders at St. Andrews. I mean, when things like that happen it must be hard to live with yourself but Dai never collapsed like that.'

Huggett, who represented Wales with Rees in the World Cup and served under his Ryder Cup captaincy in 1967, can appreciate, however, just why he fared so well in Opens.

'He had a tremendous all-round game and it was hard to find any weaknesses. I reckon his best department was the fairway woods. He was a brilliant wooden club player, which is why I think he did so well on the British links courses which house the Opens.

'Dai would hit the greens eight times out of ten with his three or four wood. He was superb off the fairway as he had the skill to control his shots.'

Brian, who became inspired as a youngster by the feats of Dai Rees, also admired his countryman's unshakeable faith in his own ability. 'Dai had a tremendous way of looking at his bad shots . . . he simply didn't believe he hit any!

'Nothing was ever his fault. He never blamed himself. If something didn't come off, it wasn't caused by Dai Rees. It was always a bad lie, or a camera clicking or some such thing. It's a great attitude to have on the golf course, really, to believe that you are the best player in the world, and it was a wonderful asset to him.'

Rees had two more close calls before age finally caught up with him. In 1954 he travelled to Birkdale six weeks early in order to survey the condition of the course before penning an article on the forthcoming Open. The grass had been allowed to grow thick and coarse at the rear of some greens and Dai said prophetically at the time: 'Someone's ball could become snagged in that stuff and it could cost him the Open'. Little did he know that he would become the unfortunate victim!

'He really did think he was going to win it that year,' recalled Eunice Rees. 'He scored exactly the same as Peter Thomson in the first three rounds, but eventually lost by a single shot to Peter.

'He knew that a par 4 at the last might be enough to win, or at least force a play-off.

And with Thomson coming up behind, he wanted to put extra pressure on the Australian. I was very upset when he took 5. David was deeply disappointed as well but didn't make a fuss about it.'

Rees, who reckoned he needed three pars to win, achieved two-thirds of that objective at the 16th and 17th. But after a perfect drive at the last his three-iron approach skipped over the green . . . and nestled in the wiry rough to which Dai had objected.

The ball lodged in a tuft of grass, demanding a miraculous chip. Rees chopped the ball out to 10 feet, but left his putt one inch away from the hole. Thomson finished with a four to clinch the trophy by one shot. Another chance gone.

His last genuine opportunity came at the age of 48, just two years short of qualification for the Seniors championship. This time only the genius and brute strength of Arnold Palmer deprived Dai of a historic victory in 1961.

After leading for the first two rounds, the resilient little Welshman found himself only one behind Arnie with 18 holes to play.

At last the title seemed bound for Wales, or more accurately the South Herts club just north of London where Dai had become professional shortly after the War.

Unfortunately Palmer chose that day to play two of the greatest recovery shots in Open history. At the 15th and 16th he bulldozed through gorse, thorns, roots and dandelions to rescue his round.

To this day, a plaque commemorating the shot at the 16th nestles half-buried in the rough at Birkdale, a lasting testimony to that superhuman achievement.

Dai needed birdies at the 17th and 18th to tie and, after narrowly missing at the penultimate hole, drilled a six iron to 10 feet and holed his putt for a birdie 3 at the last. His 72 left him one stroke behind Palmer and for the third time in his career Rees, the perennial runner-up, was bridesmaid once more.

Palmer, magnanimous to the last, reached out and shook Dai's hand and commented: 'You deserved a play-off for finishing like that'. It was a fine gesture from a true sportsman, and Dai's compensation was a cheque for £1000, his first four-figure prize in over 30 years of tournament golf.

If Rees's record in the toughest stroke-play event in the British Isles was littered with hard luck stories, he had few peers — and even fewer failures — in the highly individual art of match-play.

In the early days, Dai tended to have something of a combustible nature on the course, as he proved one day at Harrogate when he required a 10-foot birdie putt for a round of 63. The ball struck an old pitch mark and slipped past the hole. Rees, in a fit of rage, promptly snapped his offending club across one knee — and suffered the indignity of having to hole out virtually bent double with a six inch putter!

But once he had controlled the urge to explode following a missed putt or wayward shot, all that pent-up energy was channelled into winning matches.

The pre-War years had seen Dai develop the powerful physique that his 5ft 6in frame demanded, while all the time the years of punishing practice under his father's watchful eye were beginning to pay off.

'Develop striking power and iron out the kinks later,' his dad repeated constantly and Dai took the advice to heart, earning a single-figure handicap by the age of 14.

Following the move to Aberdare, he worked at his game for eight to 10 hours a day until his hands were calloused and bleeding. The living-room carpet also took a pounding from lengthy putting sessions while occasionally Dai's father made him play for his supper by keeping his ravenous son on the practice ground until he hit the green with a certain number of balls.

Soon Dai became as hungry for success as for his mum's home cooking. In 1933 he broke 70 in a tournament for the first time and qualified for the prestigious *News of the World* Match-Play, a tournament which would become synonymous with Dai Rees.

The first Match-Play title at Oxhey in 1936 underlined the short fuse which burned within Rees's sturdy frame. In the final against Ernest Whitcombe, one of the three famous golfing brothers, Dai was four down at lunch and overheard a local member declare: 'Young Rees won't reach the turn this afternoon'.

That innocuous comment provoked a frenzied reaction from Dai who not only lasted to the turn but ripped out seven threes in a nine-hole spell from the 23rd and birdied the last for victory and a £200 cheque.

Two years later, Dai's wedding present to Eunice was a second Match-Play, beating Ernie — son of Ernest — in the final. Later he also beat the inimitable Henry Cotton and Frank Jowle to win consecutive titles in 1949 and '50 before making three unsuccessful final appearances in '53, '67 and '69.

Incidentally, the Whitcombe brothers played a vital role in Dai's career during the thirties. At the time he was agonising over whether to persevere with the two-fisted 'baseball' grip or adopt a more conventional overlapping or interlocking method.

Charlie Whitcombe advised him: 'Don't consider changing unless you're unhappy with your results'. Since he had smallish hands and felt uncomfortable with the Vardon grip, Rees opted for the status quo, and seldom had reason to regret it.

The intervention of the War deprived Rees of six prime years, but neither the African campaign nor the Normandy landings could part him from his golf clubs. Between 1939 and '45 he played with King George VI, Field Marshall Montgomery and General Eisenhower thanks to his role as a driver for Air Vice Marshall Sir Harry Broadhurst.

Eunice Rees remembers: 'I was very grateful to Montgomery. He had a son at boarding school near Hindhead, where David had become pro before the War. He knew David, of course, and frequently wrote to his son telling him to go and visit Mrs Rees and say that her husband was fine!

'Actually I learned a lot about golf in those days. I used to keep the shop ticking over and I was even taught how to whip golf clubs and make minor repairs.'

The *News of the World* Match-Play first brought Dai to the attention of the British public, but the Ryder Cup turned him into a national hero.

He represented Britain and Ireland nine times between 1937 and '61 (it would have been 10 but for the 1939 cancellation) and competed in the last four as captain. Later, as his playing powers declined, he was awarded the role of non-playing captain in 1967.

From all those jousts with the Americans, Rees emerged on top only once, at Lindrick in Sheffield in 1957 when Britain and Ireland completed one of the great fightbacks in Ryder Cup history.

However, Brian Huggett is convinced Rees would have been as successful as Tony Jacklin had he been operating under today's rules and conditions. He said: 'Dai didn't have the ammunition. In those days there were six players who were good enough for the Ryder Cup and six who weren't. You can't expect to beat the Americans with half a team.

'Without the players, Dai was on a hiding to nothing, so the win in 1957 was a tremendous achievement. I came to realise at Houston in 1967 what an inspirational guy he was. He could get you going and if he had been in charge today, I think he would be classed as a really great captain.'

The captaincy of the 1955 team was 'the greatest honour of his life' according to Eunice. She said: 'Deep down, he always knew he had what it took to be captain and he tackled the job with tremendous enthusiasm, as usual.

'He had an ability to communicate, and that's why I think he was successful as a Ryder Cup captain. He also tried to understand people and unlike some golfers took the Ryder Cup in his stride.'

Britain suffered a comprehensive defeat by the Americans at the Thunderbird club in Palm Springs in 1955 but the P.G.A. retained their faith in Rees and re-appointed him as captain for the 1957 match at Lindrick.

Things didn't go according to plan on the first day at Sheffield, as the Americans sprinted into a 3-1 lead with eight singles to come. The only point had come from Rees and Ken Bousfield who beat Art Wall and Fred Hawkins 3 and 2.

Dai, absorbed in his own game, resisted the urge to rebuke his players. Max Faulkner volunteered to be dropped for the singles on account of his poor form, so the battle lines were drawn.

Eric Brown, the fiery Scot, was his trump card. Rees guessed correctly that the volatile Tommy Bolt would be the American No 1, so he decided to match fire with fire. 'You've never lost to a Yank before,' Dai told Brown, 'So don't start now. We need a good start and you can do it!'

The 'Brown Bomber' responded with a 4 and 3 victory and the home side were ahead in four matches when Rees teed up against Ed Furgol. Such was his desire to watch the rest of his team in action that Dai hammered the dazed American 7 and 6.

Britain and Ireland won six of the eight singles to register their first triumph for 24 years and Eunice Rees admitted: 'It was the most thrilling day of his life. He was so proud

The Master! Sandy Lyle launches into his version of the Highland Fling after becoming the first Briton to capture the U. S. Masters title at Augusta National.

' You little beauty '. Nick Faldo handles the Open Championship trophy with tender loving care after his triumph at Muirfield.

Victorious Ryder Cup captain Tony Jacklin and team celebrate the return of the cup to Europe for the first time in 18 years at The Belfry.

Britain Again! Nick Faldo wins the 1989 U. S. Masters.

of his team. That Ryder Cup win probably made up for all those disappointments in the Open.'

Suddenly, Dai Rees was a British institution along with bangers and mash. His popularity with the public and press won him the BBC's Sportsview Personality of the Year, the Golf Writers' Trophy and the Welsh Sportsman of the Year Award. The CBE followed in the 1958 New Year's honours list.

If the Ryder Cup in 1957 was a triumph, the 1959 renewal almost turned into tragedy as the chartered jet carrying the British and Irish team to the Palm Desert club in California plunged out of control. The journey was only a short hop from Los Angeles but the plane struck a vast air pocket and dropped 4000 feet. The entire contents of the cabin were strewn throughout the jet along with the contents of some sensitive stomachs!

'He really thought his end had come,' recalled Mrs Rees. 'He wasn't keen on flying, or even travelling on boats, but knew it had to be done if he wanted to play golf all over the world.

'On that particular occasion he was quite convinced there was no escape and absolutely hated the experience. When the plane eventually landed no-one wanted to get back on board, so a Greyhound bus was used to transport them to the golf club.

'The only good which came of that terrible day was the formation of the Long Drop Club. It was the idea of John Letters, the club maker, who was on the flight, and for many years after we all met — wives as well — for an annual dinner to toast the good luck of those on the flight.'

The United States took advantage of their opponents' threadbare nerves and won easily, as they did at Lytham in 1961. However Rees, now 48, ended his Ryder Cup playing career on an exuberant note by beating both Jay Hebert and Doug Ford in the last-day singles.

There was nowhere in the world Dai Rees would not go in order to further the game of golf, and increase the collection of silverware in the process. Apart from a host of titles won in Britain and Ireland, he was a prodigious winner overseas and twice won the Vardon Trophy for the lowest stroke average on home soil.

As the years rolled by, Dai's infectious enthusiasm for the game kept him active on the tournament scene as well as at South Herts. In the 1973 Martini at Barnton in Edinburgh, he shot rounds of 72, 70, 67 and 71 to finish second, one behind Maurice Bembridge. He was 60 years old.

His last success came in 1975 when he won the South of England P.G.A. event from a decent quality field. Not a major tournament, perhaps, but still a remarkable achievement by a remarkable golfer.

So what was the reason for his longevity in the cut and thrust of competitive golf? Eunice Rees feels it was because he was hopelessly besotted by the game. 'It was his life as well as his living. He loved the game, and had such a competitive streak that he couldn't give it up. He enjoyed winning, and unlike so many of his contemporaries on the tour, he also enjoyed teaching. He had the patience for it.

'Max Faulkner once remarked that there had to be a better way of earning a living and David was horrified to hear that. "I can't think of a better way," he replied. He was still giving lessons right up until the last day before he went into hospital.'

Sadly, Dai's illness was serious and he died in November, 1983 without the chance to transmit the wonderful Rees method to his only grandson. However, his homeland ensured that Dai's name will live forever in the valleys. In February, 1989 a Welsh Sports Hall of Fame was opened in Cardiff. Of the first 10 names in the roll of honour only one was a golfer. Not surprisingly, it was Dai Rees.

CAREER RECORD

OVERSEAS TITLES: New South Wales Open (Australia) 1951; Wisemans Tournament (New Zealand) 1952; Swiss Open 1956-59-63; Egyptian Open 1954; Belgian Open 1954.

DOMESTIC TITLES: British Assistants 1935-36; P.G.A. Match-Play 1936-38-49-50; *Yorkshire Evening News* Tournament 1939-50-51 (jt)-52-56 (jt); Silver King Tournament 1946; *Daily Mail* Tournament 1947; *News Chronicle* Tournament 1947-50; Penfold Tournament 1947 (jt); Irish Open 1948; Dunlop Masters 1950-52; Daks Tournament 1953-62 (jt); Spalding Tournament 1954; P.G.A. Close Championship 1959.

SENIORS TITLES: P.G.A. Seniors 1966.

INTERNATIONAL: Ryder Cup 1937-47-49-51-53-55-57-59-61. Wales in World Cup 1954-56-57-58-59-60-61-62-64; GB v Commonwealth 1956; GB v Europe 1958; Wales in Double Diamond 1971-72-73-75-76.

MISC: Tooting Bec Cup 1946-53 (jt); Ryder Cup captain 1955-57-59-61-67; Harry Vardon Trophy 1955-59; BBC Sportsview Personality of the Year 1957; Association of Golf Writers' Trophy 1957; Welsh Sportsman of the Year 1957; Awarded CBE 1958; P.G.A. Captain 1967-76; made honorary member of the Royal and Ancient Golf Club 1976; included in Welsh Sports Hall of Fame 1989.

4

MAX FAULKNER

THE fact that Max Faulkner won the British Open in 1951 is known to most golf aficionados. That he almost wasn't alive to compete at Royal Portrush is less well documented.

There have been few dull moments in Max's rich and varied career, but this engaging Englishman would happily have avoided a terrifying episode in 1950 which saved one life — and nearly cost him his own.

If he hadn't been born to golf, Max Faulkner might well have spent most waking hours with a fishing rod instead of a driver or a putter in his hands.

And it was that love affair with the sea, and fishing in particular, which drew Faulkner — already a leading candidate for the following year's Open — to a prime location on the rocks off Selsey Bill overlooking the English Channel on the 3rd of June, 1950.

'I used to fish for bass off the rocks,' recalled Max, 'That day my wife, Joan, was with me and as the current was so strong, she warned two young boys not to get too close to the water's edge.

'Well, they wouldn't listen and the bigger of the two lads slipped. He rolled like a top. I saw a leg, an arm then a leg again as he spun around.

'I must have been about 80 yards away but I went in and started to crawl towards the young boy, who had been caught in a sort of whirlpool where the current changed direction. Suddenly it occurred to me: "I can't do this or I'll have no strength to come back".

'So I breaststroked the rest of the way and this little chap — who was upside down when I got there — locked his arms round my neck, making it just possible to breathe. I started back, but three-quarters of the way there I was finished. I couldn't go any further.'

At that precise moment, 34-year-old Max was destined for a watery grave, and his name would have been engraved on a chunk of granite rather than golf's most prized trophy 13 months later. However, as is often the case, truth is stranger than fiction.

'I knew those rocks like the back of my hand and realised there should be an old wall just underneath the surface. I lowered my legs in 15 feet of water — and found myself standing on it.

'I was 10 to 15 yards from my wife, with the lad still gripping my throat tightly.

I regained some of my strength then gave three or four pushes to get me back to dry land.'

Joan Faulkner grabbed the youngster and revived him with hot tea, while the exhausted Max didn't even have the strength to climb out of the water.

'By now two men had arrived and my wife said: "Why don't you help him?" They replied: "We can't — we've got our best clothes on!" Can you believe that?' chuckled Max, who certainly wasn't laughing at the time.

A permanent memento to that harrowing escapade hangs in the hallway of Faulkner's picturesque old home, Moons Farm, deep in the heart of the West Sussex countryside.

At the instigation of the grateful boy's parents, Max was awarded a citation for his heroism and the golfer turned lifeguard travelled to Battersea Town Hall in London to be presented with the framed document from the Royal Humane Society in November that same year.

'Saving a life was more important than winning a golf championship,' declared Max. But winning golf tournaments was something he achieved with far greater regularity during an extraordinary career.

Born in Bexhill in Sussex in 1916, Faulkner was hitting golf balls almost before he could walk, encouraged by his father, a member of the pro ranks.

'I have a photograph of me at four years old with a swing which seems better than the one which won me the Open,' joked Max. 'Seriously, though, I was lucky in two respects — golf came absolutely naturally to me and I had a very supportive dad.'

He was also an extremely persuasive man. It is still a source of amusement to Faulkner that his father sweet-talked his school in Guildford into allowing the adolescent Max the afternoons off to practise his golf.

'I was only 14 and a half and dad went to see the headmaster. I don't know how he managed it, but he arranged for me to play in the afternoon when everyone else was in the classroom. I was very lucky, but my dad had great faith in me, even as a youngster.

'Because I was a natural golfer I never really needed to practise a lot, although I did work hard in those days. In the evenings my father and mother used to come up to the club to drag me away.

'I used to practise long after dark beside the 15th green, which was near the clubhouse at Bramley. As long as I could see the black outline of the hole in the moonlight, that was good enough for me. I used to putt in pitch darkness before my parents found me. I suppose you could say I was doing a bit of moonlighting in those days!'

Max's natural gifts were quickly translated into tangible rewards. At 12 he had entered and won a boys' tournament at Bramley, where his father had been appointed professional two years previously.

That initial success led to many more victories in the Surrey and Sussex area and at the age of 17 he took the Guildford Alliance meeting at Leatherhead.

'By this time I was playing off a handicap of two and shot 71 for a net 69. Alf Perry, who went on to win the Open a couple of years later, scored a 69 but he was playing off plus two in that meeting. So I picked up the cup and still have it to this day.'

It was becoming clear that the slender young teenager was hell-bent on a career in golf, and at the age of 17 he turned professional. 'One day my dad turned round and said he had fixed me up with an assistant's job at Sonning in Berkshire, and that was me on my way.'

However, just a few months prior to Faulkner's transfer from the amateur to the professional ranks, he was offered a sly peek into the future: a privileged opportunity to discover the unique exhilaration of playing in the Open Championship.

Although still two weeks short of his 17th birthday, Max's silver-tongued father again succeeded in pulling a few strings and his son was allowed to play in the 1932 Open at Sandwich.

'Lord knows how he fixed it!' marvelled Max. 'You couldn't play in the Open at 16 in those days but my old dad was a popular chap and he must have talked somebody into letting me enter.

'Anyway, enter I did and proceeded to shoot rounds of 77 and 78. Not bad for a first attempt. I didn't qualify for the last two rounds but I remember following Gene Sarazen, who won that year. I'll never forget the way he hit the ball and from that moment I set my heart on winning that championship.'

That craving was to be satisfied exactly 19 years later, at Royal Portrush beside the famous landmark of the Giant's Causeway in County Antrim.

It was Faulkner's first, and so far only, visit to the wonderful Irish course. It was also the solitary occasion to date that the Open Championship has ventured outside Scotland and England. But that July week in 1951, Max Faulkner and Royal Portrush were in perfect harmony.

By this time, Faulkner's bravery off the rocks at Selsey Bill was ancient history, but on the course he performed heroics with his putter — one of around 300 he has employed, and often discarded, down the years.

'Actually, I nearly won the Open in '49 at Sandwich. I rattled off scores of 71, 71, and 71 to share the lead with Bobby Locke and Harry Bradshaw, but they finished with 70s to my 74.

'I was just as consistent the following year at Troon but this time my rounds of 72, 70, 70 and 71 left me four behind Locke. By now I could taste an Open victory and when 1951 came around, I almost knew I was going to win it. I had a gut feeling. Even as a young man I knew I would make it one day and I sensed Portrush was the one.

'The astonishing thing is that Locke's scores and mine were identical for those three Opens in '49, '50 and '51 yet he won two titles to my one. I often think it could so easily have been the other way round.'

So Faulkner arrived in Ireland anticipating victory — and under a considerable amount of financial pressure to win.

'I always had a soft spot for flash cars and just before the Open I paid £1000 for this powerful machine with a V8 engine. That was a lot of money in those days and it was equally expensive to run. My last words to my wife at the airport were: "If I don't win the Open I'll have to sell this damn car!" '

When Max stepped onto the tee at Royal Portrush he was unmistakable, to say the least. In the days of cloth caps and general sober dress, he invariably cut a dashing figure in the plus twos which became his trademark and by wearing colour co-ordinated clothes.

He admitted: 'I loved to dress extravagantly. I won the Open wearing canary yellow shoes, yellow socks and trousers and blue top. I was fond of the pastel colours and I reckon I started a trend with my on-course dress.

'Mind you, there was a practical reason for wearing plus twos. When I played in strong winds I used to get irritated by my trousers flapping around my ankles as I concentrated on my putting. Once I had started wearing the plus twos, I never stopped.'

When it came to the science of putting — flapping trousers or no flapping trousers — Faulkner had few peers in his day, even although putters of all shapes and sizes used to pass through his hands before, inevitably, landing on the scrapheap.

By a stroke of luck one of those hundreds of putters came into his possession just prior to the 1951 Open. And for four days at Portrush he wielded that putter with a precision and authority seldom seen in a major championship.

Max explained the background. 'The putter was very light, only 11 ounces, with a face that was just two and a half inches long and an inch deep. The grip was also slim and it was appropriately called the pencil putter.

'Putting, to my mind, is all about feel and I gripped my putter so gently anyone could have knocked it out of my hands. Anyway, I simply loved this one and at Portrush my putting was absolutely phenomenal.

'I remember I had 27 putts in the first round, 24 in the second, 29 in the third and 29 again in the fourth. I beat 30 putts in each round and to my knowledge that has never been done before or since. It was quite extraordinary. I think if you beat 30 putts a round you can still win big tournaments playing "rough".

'Bobby Locke was so impressed he wanted me to go to the States. He reckoned I could make a packet out there but I said: "No, Bob, I've got a family in England so I'll stop here."

'My driving was very straight at Portrush but my iron play was not so good and I kept missing greens. If I hadn't been forced to rely so heavily on those putts, I reckon I could have won that Open by 10 shots.'

Faulkner began with a 71, three behind leader Jimmy Adams, but tacked on two successive scores of 70 for a three-round total of 211 . . . and a commanding six-stroke lead over the rest of the field.

Such was Max's confidence on the final day that he even tempted fate on his way to the first tee.

'As I was walking through the crowd I was stopped by a father and his young son. The dad asked if I could autograph his ball for his youngster and added: "Could you sign it Max Faulkner, Open Champion?"

'I thought: "That's a good idea. I've got a big enough lead. Why not take a chance?" Good Lord, imagine doing something like that. Only an idiot would do that! I never did anything before or since but it does underline my confidence that week.'

As events turned out, Faulkner's optimism was totally justified and a closing round of 74 was sufficient to land the title by two strokes from Argentinian Antonio Cerda — and with the rest of a top-class field strung out with the washing.

The childhood dream had become reality but there was no champagne bash for the flamboyant champion. He laughed: 'I was committed to playing cricket at my son's prep school the next day so it was straight back to London and on with the pads.'

Remarkably, Max has not been back to the scene of his glorious triumph, although he confessed that the notion appealed to him. 'A sentimental return?' he was asked. 'No, of course not. For a spot of bass fishing on the Giants Causeway,' he replied mischievously.

Sadly, the trusty old putter lasted only a few more months. During practice for the Spanish Open that same year, the head parted company with the shaft and Max went into the statutory period of mourning.

'I was broken hearted. The old shaft was made of very light steel and although I tried numerous replacements it was never quite right. The end of the head was so thin that it proved very difficult to find a shaft to fit.'

Even a spot of do-it-yourself failed to produce the perfect putter. Walking on the beach one day, Max spotted a piece of driftwood washed up by the tide — and got to work with his tool kit.

'I sliced a square out of the wood and fashioned a putter head like the style used by Arnaud Massey 60 years ago. I stuck a hickory shaft in it, hammered in a piece of lead and went out and won tournaments with it. In fact I ended up making three or four from that one lump of wood but nothing approached the quality of that Open putter.'

In the 1952 Open at Royal Lytham Faulkner, using a different putter, 'made a right old muck-up of it', according to the man himself, and he was never again a serious contender.

After that, the Open proved as elusive as the ideal putter, and in the following years his most noteworthy achievements were 12th at Carnoustie in 1953 and 10th at St. Andrews in '57.

'Oh, I had quite a few imitations of my old favourite but all of them were too heavy,' said Max sadly as if discussing a death in the family. 'When I started my defence of the title I remember coming to the second green and chipping up to three feet. And I missed it. Well, that really knocked me for six because I never missed 'em from under four feet!'

As Max's putting went into decline, his collection of putters grew to such an extent that he scarcely knew what to do with them.

'One time I received a letter from a bloke up north who had heard about my collection of putters. It seems he worked in a hospital which had a putting green in the grounds so I parcelled up a bundle of 17 or 18 and sent them off. Maybe somebody's still getting the benefit of them.'

It would certainly be fair to say that Faulkner has enjoyed a charmed life, for as well as that life-saving exhibition in 1950, he also carried a fair amount of good fortune through World War II.

In golfing terms the War was an unwelcome intrusion for, as Max observed: 'I was coming along a treat then lost six precious years.'

On a couple of occasions, however, he wondered if he would still be around to resume that promising career after joining the R.A.F. in 1939. 'There were 35 of us in the same unit who had been issued with our tropical kit and told to expect an overseas draft. One night, the sergeant rushed through the door and told myself and two other chaps that we were being posted to a secret destination and to report at seven in the morning.

'Off we went in this van with the blacked-out windows. Well, I can tell you the other 32 lads were posted to Singapore six months before it fell to the Japanese . . . while I peered out of the Black Maria and found myself staring at Wentworth Golf Club!

'By an amazing coincidence, I had been called up to guard the Home Forces G.H.Q. which was at Wentworth and had a bunker underneath the clubhouse where the likes of Churchill and Eisenhower held war cabinet meetings. And to think I could have been off to Singapore. That was a near miss!'

His second escape came while stationed at Wentworth. 'One night I was guarding the Dormie House when this bomb came whistling down and landed 50 yards away in a narrow lane. Amazingly, it failed to explode. The bomb disposal experts dug it up — it was an enormous thing — and we were all evacuated while they blew it up.

'The explosion was so fierce that I realised if it had gone up in the first place I wouldn't be here to talk about it today.'

Max survived the War — 'a bit shaky but as fit as a fiddle' — and quickly resumed his professional golf career by winning the first tournament in peacetime, the 1946 Dunlop Tournament at Southport. From earning £2 10 shillings a fortnight in the R.A.F. he was back in the big-time with a £450 cheque.

The following year he was introduced to the Ryder Cup for the first time . . . and so began a love-hate relationship with the biggest team event in golf.

In five Ryder Cup appearances for Britain and Ireland, Faulkner played eight times and only had one foursomes victory on the credit side of his ledger. However, Max took a key role in the winning of the Cup at Lindrick in 1957 — by asking to be dropped!

The home side, captained by Dai Rees, trailed the Americans 3-1 after the opening day and another defeat loomed large on the horizon. Faulkner, who had lost his foursome with Harry Weetman, knew in his heart that he was more of a handicap than a help to the team.

'I hadn't played well in that foursome, but I still felt the team could win the match.

So I went to see Dai and said: "You'd better drop me. I'm not happy with my game. Play Peter Mills in my place."

'We were great buddies and he appreciated the gesture. He replied quietly: "Thanks very much, Max, you've saved me a lot of trouble."

'Quite honestly I was delighted to be left out. I knew I wouldn't have won because of the psychological effect of my previous experiences. I had lost all my other Ryder Cup singles and didn't have the confidence to have another go while Mills was young and playing wonderfully well at the time.'

Suffice to say that Mills trounced Jackie Burke 5 and 3 as the British team won six and halved one of the eight singles to pull off a spectacular triumph.

'I don't regret the Ryder Cup defeats because I was on the winning side in '57. Instead of playing in the singles I acted as a runner. I got a notebook and pen and ran from match to match relaying information to my team-mates. I must have run six or seven miles flat out — remember there were no scoreboards in those days — and it was exhilarating just to be part of the victory.'

Max has his own theory as to why he didn't make a greater impact in the Ryder Cup. 'Frankly, I reckon I was unlucky. I played Lloyd Mangrum at his peak, I faced Sam Snead on his favourite course of Pinehurst, then, of course, there was "Dutch" Harrison.'

That ill-fated game took place at Ganton in 1949, the day after Faulkner had won his only Ryder Cup point in the foursomes along with Jimmy Adams.

'The captain, Charlie Whitcombe, put me at No 1 in the singles against Harrison. I was looking forward to it until he started with six threes in a row. I had four threes and found myself two down! No-one has ever done that to me, before or since, but that finished me. Put me right off, it did.'

Harrison went on to record an 8 and 7 win to spearhead an American success, and although Max took part in three more Ryder Cup matches, that one game left its psychological scars, just as Lee Trevino's chip-in at Muirfield sickened Tony Jacklin many years later.

Despite those unhappy moments in the Ryder Cups, Faulkner's tournament victories came thick and fast. In 1951 he captured the Dunlop Masters, enjoyed the sunshine on his back in winning the Spanish Open in '52, '53 and '57, and took the P.G.A. Match-Play Championship in '53.

But possibly the most outrageous victory of all came in Portugal in 1968, when Max was 52 years of age, and thinking seriously about retirement.

'By 1968 I had begun to wind down my tournament appearances — but I was still as tough as old boots inside! Six of the new crop of Ryder Cup players were in Estoril; blokes like Brian Barnes and Tommy Horton, and I beat the lot of them.

'I averaged 69 in that event. It was an easy course but very narrow and I had the guts to take a driver while the young fellows were cautious and taking irons off the tee. That's where I beat them. I was always a pretty straight hitter and I didn't worry about any trees.

It's very difficult to win in your fifties but I did it and the younger chaps seemed bewildered to be beaten by an old man!'

Faulkner was never one to resist a challenge, and that gambling spirit and a touch of wanderlust took him to some exotic locations.

One of his oddest possessions is a photograph taken in Egypt in 1947 — showing Max balanced precariously on the hump of a camel, hitting a golf ball off the poor beast's head.

'I had been invited by Alf Padgham to compete in the Egyptian Open somewhere near the banks of the Nile. I always liked a dare so I hit the shot. Blinking camel kept turning round and tried to bite me. In that respect it was just like a human . . . it couldn't keep its head still over a shot!'

Another trip abroad took Faulkner to Hong Kong shortly after his Open Championship victory in 1951. This time he was challenged to drive the first green, some 300 yards away.

Max recalled gleefully: 'One of our hosts, a tea planter, offered me £100 in travellers cheques if I could hit the green. Unfortunately I was a foot short but he sportingly put up the same stake if I broke the course record the following day.

'I said to him: "What's the record?" He informed me it was 71 and I replied: "Good God, I can beat that!" The next day I went round in 67 and collected the money.'

After winning two Seniors titles in 1968 and '70, Faulkner decided to wind down his golfing activities to concentrate on the more tranquil life of a country squire among his pigs and chickens down on the farm.

Money was no problem, thanks to a shrewd family investment many years before. In 1947 Max and his parents had the foresight to sink their life savings into buying Selsey Golf Club and they proceeded to develop the site.

'We cut the course from 18 holes to nine and used 20 acres as a caravan site. Eventually we received permission to build chalets so the builders moved in and we constructed 300, none of which looks directly into the other. A bar was installed along with a room for children to play in the wet weather.'

The 'holiday camp' project was so successful that Max was able to sell his interest in Selsey for a seven-figure sum at the beginning of the eighties — and sink his profits into another major project.

Max joined forces with a near neighbour, Clive Coulson, the former manager of rock groups Led Zeppelin and Bad Company, to create a brand new golf complex at West Chiltington in Sussex.

And he was able to see the ambitious plan reach fruition in February, 1989 when the 18-hole course and clubhouse were opened by Denis Thatcher, whose wife has more pressing matters than golf to occupy her time.

'I'm only the mole-catcher! That's my new job at the club,' joked Max, whose son-in-law, Ryder Cup player Brian Barnes, is the resident and touring professional at West Chiltington.

Nowadays, golf takes second place to his great passion of fishing from his own boat which is moored at Littlehampton on the south coast.

'I've had a wonderful life and wouldn't change it,' he stated emphatically. 'My only frustration is that I've been afflicted by a hereditary complaint called familial tremors. When I'm passive, nothing happens. But when I try to do something — like play golf or tie fish hooks — I start to shake.

'The important thing is that I don't need money, I have a fast car and I can rise at 5 a.m. every day to go fishing. Quite honestly, I've been so lucky that I wouldn't get wet if I fell overboard!'

CAREER RECORD

MAJOR TITLES: British Open 1951.
OVERSEAS TITLES: Spanish Open 1952-53-57; Portuguese Open 1968.
DOMESTIC TITLES: Dunlop Tournament 1946-50; Penfold Foursomes 1949; Lotus Tournament 1949; Dunlop Masters 1951; P.G.A. Match-Play 1953.
SENIOR TITLES: Pringle P.G.A. Seniors Championship 1968-70.
MISC: Ryder Cup 1947-49-51-53-57; Association of Golf Writers Trophy 1951.

5
CHRISTY O'CONNOR

I F the Irish race is truly blessed with good luck, Christy O'Connor can be excused for
asking where his share went.

Talent is one thing, application is another. But without that intangible element —
luck — even the most gifted golfers occasionally suffer from the curse of unfulfilled ambition.

Such is the case of O'Connor, or simply 'Himself' to the devoted army of followers
who recognised virtuosity when they saw it in the powerful frame of the man from Galway.

Few golfers are granted one chance to challenge for the greatest prize of them all, the
Open Championship. O'Connor was in at the 'sharp end' on a number of occasions, but
was destined to emerge empty-handed.

It is his one lasting regret in a professional career spanning more than four decades.

'The Open Championship is your pension for life,' he said wistfully. 'Winning that
title means so much more than any other, but I couldn't quite manage it.

'I was so close several times and I wonder if it just wasn't meant to be. I have
many fond memories of that championship — but the disappointments still hurt a little
even now.'

So why did that coveted Open title elude Patrick Christopher O'Connor, one of the
sweetest swingers to come from the Emerald Isle?

Some would say that the method which earned him the nickname 'wristy Christy' let
him down at crucial moments. Others argue that his putting was not as sound as it might
have been.

However, O'Connor believes it was just the mysterious force of old-fashioned bad
luck at work.

'You know, a bounce one way or the other can be the difference between winning
and losing an Open.

'Sure, I'm not looking for excuses. I just think it's true. People say you make your own
luck but I don't believe it.

'You need the breaks, the good fortune to hit a loose shot and get away with it. That's
how Opens are won and lost.'

Lady Luck was in an especially vindictive mood on one bright Saturday in July, 1958

. . . a day which was to haunt O'Connor for the rest of his life.

It was the day that 33-year-old Christy O'Connor came within a whisker of pulling off his burning ambition of holding aloft the famous old claret jug.

'I can remember it as if it was yesterday,' recalled Christy. 'Royal Lytham was one of my favourite courses and I felt in great shape during practice. I knew in my heart I could win that week.

'Sure enough, I played brilliantly in the first two rounds and shot a 67 followed by a 68 to lead the field by a stroke with the lowest halfway aggregate since Henry Cotton at Sandwich in 1934.'

However, just as the long-cherished dream came sharply into focus, the breaks started to go against O'Connor.

'In these days we had to play the final two rounds on the last day. You had to learn to skip round fast, eat fast between rounds and go back and get on with the job in the afternoon.

'Well, I was playing with an Argentinian, Leopoldo Ruiz, immediately behind Peter Thomson and Dave Thomas.

'Ruiz and myself loved to get on with it and were constantly hard on the heels of the others. It was painfully slow and my concentration wavered so much that I grabbed an R. and A. official and demanded action.

'He replied that it was me who was too quick, not Thomson and Thomas who were at fault, and told me to slow down myself! Needless to say I was furious and struggled to an unconvincing 73.'

The final round followed the same pattern, but Christy held his game together tenaciously and arrived at the 72nd hole requiring a par 4 to tie — or a birdie 3 to win.

At that moment, he believes his chance evaporated, and all because of the chaotic crowd scenes one usually associates with the climactic moments of an Open Championship.

As the spectators pushed and jostled for a better vantage point to watch the last two combatants on the course, O'Connor and Ruiz were left with a rapidly shrinking fairway ahead of them.

'We had to wait on that 18th tee for what seemed like an eternity,' said Christy. 'Of course it wouldn't happen today with the strict stewarding policy. The crowds would have been behind ropes.

'But the people simply wouldn't get back on the left and Ruiz and I were left with half a fairway to aim at! Despite these handicaps we hit our drives anyway.

'Looking back I think the crowd may have ruined my chance. I hit a good shot with a three wood but saw nothing as the spectators surged forward.

'Imagine how I felt when I found the ball in the fairway bunker alongside Ruiz's. He took two shots to get out so I took the sensible course and splashed out to ensure I didn't make the same mistake.'

But the damage was done. Christy pitched to 15 feet and his putt to tie hovered agonisingly on the lip of the cup. A bogey 5 — and the dream was over.

A final round of 71 left O'Connor in a tie for third place with Eric Brown on 279, a single stroke behind Thomas and the eventual champion Thomson, who won the 36-hole play-off.

'That really hurt,' remarked Christy, wincing at the painful memory. 'I was very disappointed. I would love to have won the Open, and if I had done so that year, I reckon I would have won it again.

'That message keeps coming back to me. I'm sure that if I'd broken that mental barrier, anything might have been possible.'

Three years earlier O'Connor had also threatened to capture the title at St. Andrews before, quite literally, going to Hell and back!

Teeing off in the final round, his prospects of catching Peter Thomson were remote. After scores of 71, 75 and 70 the Irish maestro was seven strokes adrift and could have been excused for letting his mind drift to the boat trip home to wife Mary whom he had married just nine months previously.

St. Andrews may have been the cradle of golf, but Christy showed scant respect for the revered Scottish links and charged into contention with some glorious shot-making.

'I remember I was playing along with John Jacobs. The two of us simply went mad around the "loop" of the Old Course. By the time we reached the long 14th I had picked up five or six birdies and John wasn't far behind.

'At that moment I had visions of being Open champion, which of course was the kiss of death.

'I cracked a great drive down the middle and wanted to use my driver off the fairway. I could play that club magnificently off the fairway. No trouble at all.

'I asked for the driver but my caddie said "No, no, no" and tried to talk me into using a three wood. We ended up having a slanging match in the middle of the fairway — before I got my way.'

Sadly, the altercation disrupted Christy's concentration and he fluffed his second into the notorious Hell Bunker guarding the route to the 14th green.

'I was unplayable up against the face of the bunker,' he explained. 'There was no option but to try to play out backwards. It took me two efforts to escape and I was so shattered that I ran up an 8. Goodbye Open title!'

Instead of the 65 he had mentally awarded himself, Christy was forced to settle for a 71 and 10th place.

To make his discomfort more acute he was then approached on the next tee by a forlorn figure who introduced himself as a priest — who just happened to have backed O'Connor at the rewarding odds of 100-1.

Although he may have been a man of the cloth, Christy reckons 'Father X' was as close as he might ever get to blasphemy at that precise moment his financial investment disappeared in the depths of Hell!

In fact, the clergy in Ireland took O'Connor to their hearts over the years, so much so that they earned their own nickname.

During an era in which Frank Sinatra, Dean Martin and Sammy Davis, Junior were given the sobriquet of the 'Rat Pack', the sombre attire of O'Connor's religious followers resulted in them becoming known as the 'Black Pack'.

No one could ever accuse O'Connor of being a manufactured player, and his relaxed, smooth swing allied to an ability to perform miracles with a golf ball endeared him to the sport's purists.

It wasn't just the clergy who adopted him either.

'Oh, I had a tremendous following all over the British Isles. I still have,' he said fondly. 'In the old days they came out and followed you, rain or snow. I can remember hearing the raincoats flapping around as I was hitting my shots.

'Even now, in my sixties, I still get Christmas cards and letters. I suspect the reason is that I mixed a great deal with the public in those days.

'Because I lived in Ireland, I usually stayed in England or Scotland for two or three weeks at a time to play in tournaments. When others went home, I socialised.'

He added with a wicked grin: 'I did enjoy a good "jar" and liked to chat to people about golf.'

As well as the odd drink or two, Christy also had, and still has, the penchant for cigarettes — a habit which had a minor role to play in honing his game.

Life as an assistant professional was tough in the post-war years after the 22-year-old O'Connor joined the paid ranks in 1946, and time to practise was as miserly as the wages.

'Usually, by the time I had finished all my chores and given lessons during the winter months it was almost dark.

'I knew that hard work was the only way to become a tournament player so I would go down to the practice ground and drop a few dozen balls around the green.

'I always enjoyed a smoke so I placed the lighted cigarette butts onto the green then used the glow as the target for my little pitches! Not exactly recommended, but I always felt the short game was the most vital area to keep polished.'

But back to the Open Championships, and unfortunately, the prayers of the enthusiastic 'Black Pack' supporters were never answered as other potential winning opportunities came and went.

In 1959 at Muirfield, O'Connor would have scratched because of illness had it not been for the importance of the championship. He closed with an immaculate 69 for a share of fifth place, four behind an aspiring newcomer, Gary Player.

Two years later he finished joint third alongside Neil Coles after a roller-coaster ride at Royal Birkdale. Christy's third round 67 was the lowest of the week, but indifferent scores of 77 and 73 in his second and fourth rounds proved expensive.

At the age of 40, and back in Lancashire at Birkdale, the popular Irishman exploded off his blocks with a 69 but sagged in the middle by attaching a 74 and 73 to that opening effort.

A closing 71 earned him a tie for second — his highest placing — just two strokes behind the Australian who had become a regular thorn in the flesh, Peter Thomson.

There was to be only one more close call, in 1969, when British golf hailed a youthful new hero in Tony Jacklin.

However, early in the championship O'Connor resumed his passionate love affair with that most demanding of mistresses — Royal Lytham. A tortuous track to many, but a course where the cream invariably rises to the top.

'Although I was almost 45 by then, I reckoned I was in with a shout,' insisted Christy. 'By this time, the R. and A. had amended the Open format and instead of the 36-hole cavalry charge on the last day, the championship was played over four days.'

That civilised arrangement came as a welcome bonus for a middle-aged golfer whose legs and ankles ached constantly from the strain of hitting thousands of shots off bone-jarring links courses down the years.

After a solid 71 to launch the championship, Christy then ripped out one of the greatest rounds of his career, a six under par 65 and new course record for the Lancashire links.

That placed him one shot behind New Zealander Bob Charles with a halfway aggregate of 136, two ahead of the new whizzkid Jacklin.

'The fact that I didn't have to play two rounds on the same day encouraged me greatly, and that round of 65 sent my confidence soaring.

'But I began to miss some crucial putts, and none more so than at the sixth on the last day. I three-putted for a par and eventually had to settle for fifth place, four strokes behind Tony Jacklin.'

From that moment Christy ceased to be a genuine contender for the ultimate goal in golf, but continued to enter the Open until his final appearance in 1979 (where else but at Lytham?).

In all, he competed in the toughest test in golf 26 times between his debut in 1951, as an ambitious assistant pro at Bundoran, and that final occasion at Lytham in 1979, aged 54.

On seven occasions O'Connor finished in the top six, a phenomenal achievement in such a competitive environment.

'I think my record is a long way ahead of most of my contemporaries. I didn't win but I feel I didn't do badly. Disappointments are terrible things to handle, and the Open taught me that you get plenty of them!'

In view of the fact that the O'Connor family home stood on the boundary of Galway Golf Club, it was scarcely surprising that the little 'boy next door' should develop a passion for the game at an early age.

'I believe it really helps if you're born near a course,' declared Christy. 'It gives you a head start in the game. It might not make you an Open champion, but it helps.'

In those days, young Christy caddied to bring in extra money to the household — and first showed the steady nerve and gambling instinct which was to stand him in good stead in later life.

'If there was a cracking Western showing at the local cinema, all my friends and I wanted to see it. The trouble was, not all of us could afford to go.

'So we used to pool our resources, and held chipping competitions to decide who should go. By God, it was a hard school all right, but I can safely say I was something of an authority on the Wild West!'

As O'Connor grew physically, so did his reputation as a skilled practitioner with every club in the bag. And once he was even asked to prove it.

The story, he claimed, modestly, has become wildly exaggerated over the years, although it is one he clearly relishes re-telling.

'I was involved in a regular fourball at Bundoran when we came to a par 3 of just over 200 yards.

'I knocked my tee shot onto the green and my partner, who clearly had plenty faith in my ability, boasted to our opponents that I could hit the green again — using any club in the bag.

'He said "Go on, Christy, show them!" So I did. The story goes that I hit the green every time, and even holed out once!

'However, the truth is that I was accurate with most of my shots, but missed with a few. Still, it wasn't bad to do that with clubs like a sand wedge and putter.'

Remarkably, O'Connor's tournament career did not take off until he had reached the age of 30. In other sports he would already have been on the way down, but like many golfers he was just beginning to approach the peak of his physical powers.

The early signs were far from encouraging. Between 1951 and '54, his official P.G.A. earnings totalled a meagre £327, not nearly enough to sustain a new bride and trips across the Irish Sea.

However, the breakthrough arrived in 1955. The Swallow Penfold tournament offered the first £1000 prize in European golf — and Christy walked off with the cheque in his pocket.

In those days, the unknown young Irishman was forced to endure the tortuous pre-qualifying ritual, and he just squeezed into the field thanks to a 70 — including two eagles — in his second qualifying round.

O'Connor went from strength to strength and lifted his first important title by two strokes from Eric Brown, who was soon to become one of his greatest friends.

From that moment, the name of Christy O'Connor was engraved on countless trophies, most notably the P.G.A. Match-Play, Dunlop Masters (twice) and the John Player Classic in 1970 where he collected a £25,000 cheque — the biggest of his career.

Money, or an acute shortage of it, was a major factor behind O'Connor's late development as a tournament player. Interestingly, he also feels that it contributed significantly towards Great Britain and Ireland's lack of success in Ryder Cup matches against the United States.

'Looking back, I was glad I played my golf two or three decades ago. It was a great era. But I can also see that, if I had been around today, I might have been a millionaire.

'That would have given me the security I craved in the old days and which hindered our chances of beating the Americans.

'You see, I had a family depending on me in Dublin and one bad year on the tour and you were in trouble financially. You needed a second job to keep things ticking over.'

That also had an undesirable spin-off in Ryder Cup years, more of which later.

'The British and Irish golfers were very good, but we had two jobs. We were club pros as well as tournament pros. That was the big difference between the Yanks and ourselves.

'Sure it was asking too much of us. There we were giving lessons one day, rushing off to play on the tour and trying to get back to the club on Friday night.

'Tournaments used to finish on Fridays then and we had to be back to give lessons throughout the weekend before starting all over again on the Monday.

'Do you think the Americans went through the same grind? Not a chance! They were tournament professionals only. Nowadays we have some wonderful players and so they should be. They have nothing else to do but practise and play.'

The main objection O'Connor holds against today's generation is the greed which has surfaced from the presence of so much money in the game.

'My wife and I had to arrange my contracts which, frankly amounted to virtually nothing. Today these guys are on enormous contracts and getting ridiculous appearance money.'

That last subject is an emotive issue, as far as Christy is concerned: 'I think it's rotten! The payment of appearance money is ruining golf.

'I don't feel that any top pro should be awarded money simply for turning up. If he's good enough, the money's there for him to win.

'He should prove it on the battlefield. More often than not, the man who gets the money wins the first prize anyway. I don't think it's right, and many of my contemporaries feel the same way — and not out of envy, I might add.'

So to the Ryder Cup, that biennial locking of horns with the Americans which has conjured up so many moments of high drama down the years.

Only one golfer from Britain and Ireland has played in 10 matches . . . and that is Christy O'Connor.

Between his debut at Palm Springs in 1955 to his swansong at Muirfield in 1973, Christy took part in a total of 35 individual ties, winning 11, losing 20 and halving 4.

The pinnacle, unquestionably, came at Lindrick in Sheffield in 1957 when old Sam Ryder's legacy to golf was captured for the first time since 1933.

'Lindrick was fantastic. A dream. I was playing in my second Ryder Cup and we weren't expected to win.

'After the first day it certainly appeared that we wouldn't have a look in when we trailed 1-3 with only the singles to play.'

In those days, Ryder Cup ties were contested over 36 holes, and that extended format was to prove crucial to Britain and Ireland's fightback.

Christy had been placed at No 7 (out of eight) in the singles order of play and drew the promising young American with the all-American name of Dow Finsterwald.

Things went badly for the Irishman, who went into lunch trailing Finsterwald and apoplectic about the inconsistency of his putting.

'I marched off the 18th green, grabbed a quick snack and a beer then headed for the pro's shop and said "Give me a few putters".

'Well, I tried out a couple on the practice green and eventually opted for the one which gave me the best feel. Would you believe I started the afternoon round birdie, birdie — sinking two nice putts with my new putter.'

The magic wand continued to weave a spell over Finsterwald, who lost his cool (and the 21st hole) when angrily hooking the ball back on the green while it was still in motion.

'He was livid,' chuckled Christy. 'I ended up having a putt to reach the turn in 31 and although that stayed out, I won the next two holes for a 7 and 6 win. It was immensely satisfying because Harry Bradshaw, bringing up the rear, halved with U.S. Open champion Dick Mayer. We had won.'

Britain and Ireland had tamed 'Uncle Sam' in the singles by the stunning margin of 6-1 to triumph 7-4 with one game halved.

Twelve years later O'Connor contributed two and a half points out of four in the famous tied match at Royal Birkdale, where Jack Nicklaus proved himself to be a great sportsman as well as a great golfer by conceding Tony Jacklin a little teaser on the last.

'What a gesture,' observed Christy with a disbelieving shake of his head. 'You know, I first remember meeting Nicklaus when he played in England for the first time in 1962 in the Piccadilly No 1 tournament . . . and he missed the cut.

'The greens were like rocks but it didn't take him long to work out how to handle the British conditions. I honestly don't think he is much better than a lot of other players. It was just that his concentration is miraculous.'

At the ripe old age of 48 years, eight months and 30 days, O'Connor bowed out of Ryder Cup competition with a half against Tom Weiskopf, and two decades of unbroken involvement were over.

By this time, Christy's tournament victories had begun to dry up, although there were soon to be rich pickings in the world of Seniors golf.

But as he logged up his half-century to join the 'old boys' network, he could look back on many memorable moments.

There was a Canada Cup (now World Cup) win with Harry Bradshaw in Mexico in 1958 during one of 15 appearances he made in the event.

He also took possession of The Harry Vardon Trophy, as European Order of Merit leader, in 1961 and '62 and the Association of Golf Writers Award in 1977.

But the most poignant moment came in 1970 when he was made a Freeman of Galway (following in the footsteps of several presidents, cardinals and an ex-Mayor of New York).

'That was one of the biggest honours. Maybe the biggest. I was very proud and moved by it.'

However, on the golf course, there were still trophies to be won.

In 1976 he picked up the first of six P.G.A. Seniors titles and the same season won the World Seniors, which he retained the following year before the championship was discontinued.

He attempted to break into the American Seniors circuit — 'money for old rope!' — but found it to be a closed shop.

Nowadays Christy is content to play a couple of 'bounce' games each week at Royal Dublin where he is an honorary life member. 'I can still knock it round in under par in good weather,' he insisted.

Christy O'Connor is still madly in love with the game of golf and his twin sons, Peter and Christopher, have inherited some of the old magic. Both are assistant professionals, Peter at Royal Dublin and Christopher at Elm Park.

He has crammed a vast amount into a distinguished career, but the lingering regret remains that failure to win an Open.

Now if only he had had a little luck of the Irish . . .

CAREER RECORD

DOMESTIC TITLES: Swallow-Penfold Tournament 1955; Dunlop Masters 1956-59; Spalding Tournament 1956 (jt); P.G.A. Match-Play 1957; Daks Tournament 1959; Ballantine Tournament 1960; Irish Hospitals Tournament 1960-62; Carling-Caledonian Tournament 1961; Martini International 1963 (jt)-64; Jeyes Tournament 1964; Carrolls International 1964-66-67-72; Senior Service Tournament 1965; Gallaher Ulster Tournament 1966-68-69; Alcan International 1968 (jt); Bowmaker Tournament 1970; John Player Classic 1970; Ulster Professional Championship 1953-54; Irish Professional Championship 1958-60-61-62-63-65-66-71-75-77; Irish Dunlop Tournament 1962-65-66-67.

SENIORS TITLES: World Seniors Championship 1976-77; P.G.A. Seniors Championship 1976-77-79-81-82.

INTERNATIONAL: Ryder Cup 1955-57-59-61-63-65-67-69-71-73; Ireland in World Cup 1956-57-58-59-60-61-62-63-64-66-67-68-69-71-75; Ireland in Double Diamond 1971-72-73-74-75-76-77.

MISC: Harry Vardon Trophy 1961-62; Association of Golf Writers Trophy 1977.

6
ERIC BROWN

THE Ryder Cup can play strange tricks on a golfer. Like a potent drug, it has the power to stimulate the senses — or render them practically useless.

Eric Brown was one of the lucky ones who revelled in conflict. In his mind no challenge was insurmountable, no shot too difficult and no opponent unbeatable. Especially an American opponent.

No-one in Ryder Cup history can match Brown's achievement of winning all four singles matches for Great Britain and Ireland, against some of the heaviest artillery the United States could roll out.

Later, as captain, he instilled that all-consuming will to win into his team in the famous halved match at Royal Birkdale in 1969 and again at St. Louis, Missouri, two years later.

Tragically, Eric Brown died in March, 1986, at his home in Edinburgh. He was only 61, but a life lived at breakneck speed in the fast lane finally caught up with him.

Brown's widow Joan believes his enduring epitaph will be: 'He was a hell of a man!' and hopefully this chapter will be able to convey that popular impression.

Few golfers knew, or understood, the man known as the 'Brown Bomber' better than his old rival and frequent sparring-partner, John Panton.

'He was one of the best, all right,' recalled Panton, who enjoyed many epic battles with Brown during the fifties when both men were at the peak of their powers. 'When he was at the top he was as good as anybody, and that includes the fellows from overseas.

'Nowadays he would be described as a "streak" player. He had the ability to turn in some phenomenally low scores when he was playing well.

'Strangely, when he was driving well he hit the ball harder. And the harder he hit it the straighter it flew. That isn't usually the case but, of course, with Eric, nothing was ever predictable.'

Almost since the day he was born in Edinburgh on the 15th of February, 1925, Eric Chalmers Brown made a habit of doing the unexpected, and never more so than in the heat of Ryder Cup battle.

Often abrasive, occasionally irascible and always fiercely competitive, Brown cultivated a phoney 'hatred' of Americans over the years which earned him a few enemies to go with his countless friends.

In truth, what many observers interpreted as hate was simply an intense desire to beat American golfers in an age when British successes were rare.

He believed there was nothing wrong with proving that Britain could compete with the U.S.A. — or rubbing American noses in the dirt whenever possible.

'The Americans are supposed to be golf's master race,' Brown once observed impishly. 'They deserve to be knocked off their pedestal.'

No-one, to date, has achieved that ambition with such dramatic success as Eric Brown during four consecutive Ryder Cup appearances between 1953 and '59.

Despite failing to win a single point in foursomes golf, Brown positively thrived in man-to-man combat and emerged with a 100% record from brushes with America's finest.

On his debut at Wentworth in 1953, Brown played — by his own reckoning — the finest match of his life to defeat ex-United States Open Champion Lloyd Mangrum by two holes.

Next to tumble was Jerry Barber, soon to win the U.S.P.G.A., at Palm Springs before Brown sparked Great Britain and Ireland's revival in the historic 1957 victory at Lindrick with a 4 and 3 win over Tommy Bolt.

The Americans took their revenge at Palm Desert in California two years later . . . but still no-one could master the tough Scot. Eric may have been born and bred in Edinburgh, but he was endowed with the grim, pugnacious qualities of a Glasgow street-fighter.

Dr Cary Middlecoff, who went on to capture two U.S. Opens and a Masters jacket, was Brown's fourth and last Ryder Cup victim.

Britain and Ireland lost the singles 5-1 and the match by the margin of 7-2 with three games halved. Eric Brown, handed the role of 'tail gunner' by captain Dai Rees, secured the solitary point with a 4 and 3 win.

Years later Brown offered a brief glimpse into his psyche during an interview relating to the Ryder Cup captaincy. 'Once you get your man by the throat,' he said, 'you can bite a wee bit deeper and kill him off'.

Eric Brown seldom bit off more than he could chew. In those four Ryder Cup singles he was never behind at any point — a remarkable feat in view of the fact that all matches were played over 36 holes in those days.

John Panton feels that that record may never be surpassed or even equalled. He observed: 'What Eric achieved is outstanding. Remember he was playing against some of the greatest American golfers of that time, twice on their home soil.

'To win four singles takes a lot of doing — to do so over 36 holes is an even harder feat. Nowadays, over 18, you can get a flying start then hang in and hope your opponent becomes frustrated. All you need to do is hole a putt or two early on.

'Playing over 36 holes should eliminate the freak result. It's the same in snooker. There are a lot of strange results in those best-of-nine-frame sprints. But the longer the game, the better it suits the good player. How often does Steve Davis lose over the long matches?'

Not one of Brown's American opponents managed to get his measure over these marathon matches, which suited the Scot's extrovert but often prickly nature.

His first brush with Ryder Cup golf, at Wentworth in 1953, began inauspiciously. British team captain Henry Cotton had favoured an all-Scots foursome pairing on the first day but Brown and Panton were soundly thrashed 8 and 7 by Mangrum and Sam Snead.

'That was like waving a red rag in front of the bull,' chuckled Panton. 'Nothing was better designed to bring out the competitor in Eric than a beating such as the one we sustained.'

But just in case he needed it, Brown received another incentive before going out the next day to tackle Mangrum, winner of the U.S. Open seven years previously.

Joan Brown recalled: 'Henry Cotton was not at all pleased by the performance of Eric and John in the foursomes and he made some remark to the effect that he didn't expect a point from him in the singles.

'It was probably Henry's way of getting Eric wound up — and it was certainly effective. His attitude was: "Right, I'll show him" and it couldn't have worked better.'

Cotton's psychology, if that's what it was, was the motivation Brown required to secure a two-hole win in a match which was fraught with tension, but not without its moments of light relief.

Mangrum, the American Ryder Cup captain that year, clearly felt that the torture he and Snead had inflicted on Brown and Panton would be repeated in the singles.

But when the Scot covered the Burma Road course in 69 each time, he was to discover otherwise. Brown won the match — and a battle of wits.

Standing on the last tee in the second round, Brown was dormie one up and Mangrum decided the time was ripe for a spot of gamesmanship.

As Brown addressed his ball, he became aware of the American's vivid yellow jersey moving into focus out of the corner of his eye. With an icy glare, Eric turned and said calmly, 'I canny have you there, Lloyd. Just come round and stand over here where I can see you'.

Furious at the rebuke, Mangrum took a five at the last, leaving Brown needing two putts for the hole and three for the match from seven yards.

He putted up to 14 inches, but instead of receiving the congratulatory handshake was met instead with a snarl. 'I guess you can get down in two from there but let's see you do it anyway,' said the American.

Brown, a showman to the last, retorted: 'You must be expecting me to drop down dead!' and to the amusement of the large gallery, then proceeded to stalk his putt, surveying all the angles, before rapping in the ball for a two-hole victory. Eric Brown, Ryder Cup hero, was born.

Despite winning the singles series 4-3, Britain and Ireland lost the Ryder Cup match by the narrow margin of 6-5 with one halved.

Two years later, at Palm Springs, Brown played indifferently in the foursomes with Syd Scott and brilliantly in the singles by beating Barber 3 and 2.

The Ryder Cup had been in America's possession for 24 years before the biennial match teed off at Lindrick in Sheffield in 1957. It was to be one of the highlights of Brown's career and stamped him as a golfer of the highest calibre.

Once again, his distaste for foursomes became apparent when he and his great pal, Christy O'Connor, were hammered 7 and 5 by Dick Mayer and Tommy Bolt as the Americans established a 3-1 first-day lead.

However, captain Dai Rees refused to be concerned and played Eric at No 1 against the formidable 'Thunder' Bolt. That confidence was repaid in full when Brown charged into a four-hole lead at lunch and went on to win by 4 and 3.

That victory set the mood for the rest of the British and Irish team and a wave of infectious confidence spilled right through the line-up. The home team won six of the eight singles by crushing margins to wrest the Cup from the Americans.

But if Ryder Cup golf was the making of Eric Brown the golfer, it may have been responsible for the breaking of Eric Brown, the man.

Dogged by illness and injury for much of his adult life, the deterioration of his health seems to have been due, at least in part, to the burden of captaining the Ryder Cup team on two occasions.

He proved to be a born leader and a 'natural' for the job, but it was not the sort of work for a man who was known to have an irregular heart-beat, had suffered minor strokes, back trouble and was prone to fibrositis and arthritis.

'Being captain was the most exciting period of Eric's life,' declared Joan Brown. 'But it took a tremendous amount out of him. There was so much to do, so many things to organise.

'Eric took the captaincy very seriously and it became an obsession. During the matches it was a 24 hours a day involvement and he hardly slept at all. He wanted to make certain that everything was right for the team.'

Brown also alluded to the stresses of Ryder Cup captaincy some years later. Following the near miss in St. Louis he said: 'When I returned from Missouri I was shattered. I'd been up at six every morning and getting back to the hotel at eight in the evening. Eventually I was convinced I had ulcers!'

Brown's 'work hard, play hard' philosophy earned him a reputation as a hellraiser, a rebel and a troublemaker but he commanded, and demanded, loyalty right through his life.

John Panton, a master of understatement, remembered: 'Yes, he was a wee bit aggressive. He always spoke his mind and sometimes blew his top on the spur of the moment. Often he was right, but occasionally I think he regretted a few of his outbursts.

'If you were a friend of Eric he was totally loyal towards you. He wouldn't let you down. We were different in that Eric was an extrovert and I was the shy one, but we became firm friends.

'A lot of people have said this, but I think it is probably true — Eric Brown needed a little of John Panton in him, while John Panton could have used a touch of Eric Brown!'

Joan Brown added: 'He did cross people and it was unfortunate if they couldn't take it. However, he never said anything to be deliberately nasty to a person.

'He had a very fiery, quick temper all right, but it blew over in no time. He never bore a grudge or went into the huff. One minute he would be upset and the next he would snap out of it and say: "Right, let's have a party". That's the sort of man he was.

'Golf was there to be played. It was a game to be enjoyed first, a vehicle for making money second. Sometimes Eric didn't even know how much he was playing for. He was often asked: "How much did you win?" and he would reply: "I haven't a clue".

'Eric never had a cash register mind. As long as he had some money in his pocket he was happy. In fact he used to say: "I would rather die owing a million than owning a million!" That was his attitude to life. He lived for today.'

The legendary competitiveness surfaced during Brown's schooldays in Bathgate, where the family had moved when Eric was a toddler.

And it was an incident at school which prevented Brown from being lost to the ranks of professional golf for ever.

A natural all-rounder, Eric had swept the boards in the school sports and was handed the anchor leg in the 4 x 400-yard relay to complete the programme.

Joan took up the story: 'Eric had about 20 yards to make up when he was handed the baton. But he was so determined to win the relay that he ran himself into the ground. Everything went into it.'

Needless to say, Brown breasted the tape first . . . before collapsing in a heap. His father had to carry him home and it was discovered that the youngster had sustained some lung damage.

'That summed up the way Eric ran his life,' reflected Joan sadly. 'It was probably what killed him in the end. He did most things to excess.

'He liked a drink, and had a strong head and stomach for it in his young days. He also smoked too much which didn't do him any good. A combination of these circumstances, and his erratic heart-beat, probably led to the strokes.'

But for that moment on the school playing field, Brown would probably have been a policeman on patrol at Tynecastle Park in Edinburgh, the home of his first love, Heart of Midlothian Football Club.

In 1946, after winning the Scottish Amateur title at his first attempt, Eric had become disillusioned with the idea of professional golf after 17 job applications were rebuffed.

Instead, he opted for a career with Edinburgh City Police, passed the entrance examinations and had even taken the oath when he was asked to take a routine X-ray. The picture revealed an inactive scar on one of his lungs, a legacy of that lung-bursting relay race several years earlier.

That physical flaw closed the door on a career of law enforcement, but the police force's loss was golf's gain.

Had it not been for failing that medical, Eric Brown would probably not have been pounding the beat at Royal Birkdale and St. Louis as the Ryder Cup captain in 1969 and '71.

The British and Irish selectors realised that, whatever Brown's shortcomings in the field of diplomacy, he would be a committed and aggressive leader. So it proved at Birkdale in the September of '69.

After two days of foursome and four-ball play, the match was delicately poised at 6-6 with four games halved. The occasion called for a spark of ingenuity, and it duly arrived from Brown.

Tony Jacklin had just won the British Open and was clearly Britain's No 1. On the American side, The Golden Bear, Jack Nicklaus, was in his prime.

Instead of placing Jacklin midway down the 'batting order' and so virtually ensuring a couple of valuable points in the singles, Brown went for the jugular.

In both the morning and afternoon matches, Jacklin was paired with Nicklaus, winning the first encounter 4 and 3, then securing the crucial half in one of the most thrilling finishes to any Ryder Cup.

Jacklin, by courtesy of Nicklaus's generous concession on the final green, had taken one and a half points from the greatest living golfer, and Brown had shown himself to be a shrewd and inspirational captain.

However, the match did little to foster good relations between Brown and the Americans, who were aware of his apparent antipathy towards them.

In the days before the clash, Brown sparked a cold war between the sides when he was reported as saying that he had forbidden his players to help search for their opponents' balls in the rough.

Afterwards, Brown claimed his comments had been misinterpreted and his widow, Joan, is determined to set the record straight.

'That story was one which really hurt Eric and me — and damaged Eric's reputation,' she said. 'His comments were taken out of context and the story was never corrected properly in Eric's lifetime, which is sad.

'What actually happened is that the P.G.A. secretary approached Eric and said: "Could you make the boys aware of the fact that if they look for the Americans' balls and accidentally stand on one, or interfere with one in any way, we lose the hole".

'Eric told the players to be careful but the story came out twisted. Arnold Palmer got to hear of it and was very upset. After the match, when a few drinks were taken, he growled at Eric: "I don't like your attitude" and they ended up arguing.

'He was always the fairest of people on the golf course. He had a great eye for a ball and usually knew where it went. He always helped to hunt for someone's ball, even if it hurt him to find it.'

Brown was re-appointed for the 1971 match in Missouri, which ended in the best performance by a British and Irish team on American soil prior to the 1987 triumph.

But the frosty relations between Brown and his American rivals had not thawed much in the intervening two years.

On the eve of the contest, the cheerleaders were on hand for the flag-raising ceremony. However, as the rain lashed down, Eric flatly refused to allow proceedings to go ahead as planned. 'There's no way my boys are going to stand out there in the rain,' he insisted. They didn't, and once again Brown inflamed American tempers.

From the moment he swung a club at the age of four, it was clear that Eric was naturally gifted. At eight he went round Bathgate in 124 and at 13 became the youngest winner of the West Lothian boys' title.

He went to work on the railways at the age of 17, stoking fireboxes on locomotives, and took the Scottish Amateur crown at Carnoustie four years later.

With £30 from his mum to replace the set of clubs he had owned since he was 15, Brown eventually turned professional in 1946 . . . and landed headlong into the first of numerous rows with the P.G.A.

The rebel in Brown surfaced when he was forced to suffer the P.G.A.'s closed shop policy, which meant he could not take prize-money from British tournaments for five years.

Brown regarded that mandatory period as iniquitous and protested loudly and often to the golfing hierarchy, adding to his growing reputation as a firebrand.

To compensate for lack of income from tournaments he sought an alternative abroad. It was a profitable exercise and Brown went on to win the Swiss Open (on his honeymoon) as well as the Italian, Irish and Portuguese Open Championships.

But there was only really one Open which mattered to Eric Brown. The British Open.

Unfortunately, the title eluded him, but not before he had graced the competition with some of the most glorious shot-making in the post-war history of the event.

In successive years, at St. Andrews in '57 and Royal Lytham in '58, Brown completed halves of 30 and posted a marvellous score of 65 at the latter course . . . but, to his lasting regret, he failed to enter the winner's enclosure.

On both occasions he finished third, but the most bitter moment came at Lytham when he took a double bogey 6 at the last to miss out on the title by one shot.

Brown was later to remark: 'I felt awful. If it had gone well my whole life would have been different. So many avenues would have opened up; the money would have rolled in, for being Open champion is something special'.

In those days, the leaders were not necessarily out last and Brown — who started the third round eight strokes adrift — surged into contention with a record-equalling 65, thanks to an inward half of 30.

Anyone who knows the hazards lurking on that inward nine at Lytham will appreciate the brilliance of that effort: 3, 4, 2, 3, 4, 4, 3, 4, 3 = 30.

Now Eric was only three shots behind Peter Thomson. In the afternoon he kept the rhythm going and arrived at the 72nd hole ahead of his principal rivals, but guessing that a birdie 3 might clinch the title.

A booming drive caught the bunker and lodged in the face. Two more shots to reach the green, then three putts. Six.

Brown retreated to the sanctuary of his car to tune into the radio account of his Open dream reaching a sorry end. O'Connor matched his total of 279 but Thomson and Dave Thomas finished one ahead on 278 and the title had slipped away again.

Over the years, the Scot had proved himself to be a good starter but bad finisher. Twice joint leader at halfway and once outright lead after 36 holes, his highest finish was third.

That was the case at St. Andrews in 1957 where, for two hours on the opening day, he produced the most stunning golf of his life.

Brown opened with four straight birdies, missed a 'tiddler' on the fifth for another birdie and reached the turn in 30 blows: 3, 3, 3, 3, 5, 3, 4, 3, 3.

Another birdie 3 followed at the 12th and Eric was seven under par for the round. Sadly he ran up a double bogey 6 at the 13th and, in his own words, 'the magic was gone'.

A score of 67 seemed scant reward for such an exhilarating exhibition and further rounds of 72, 73 and 71 left him with a final total of 283, one behind Peter Thomson and four adrift of new champion Bobby Locke.

According to John Panton, Locke was the only golfer he saw who was capable of matching Brown on the greens.

'Eric was always a tremendous holer-out, second only to Locke. But whereas Locke took plenty of time, Eric just walked up and knocked them into the hole, seemingly without lining up.

'He didn't study the putts, especially the four, five, six footers. Locke was the best putter I ever saw. He could read the grass like nobody's business, but on his day, Eric was unstoppable. I think that explained his ability to shoot phenomenal scores.'

Around that time, Brown was more and more prone to attacks of fibrositis, a legacy of his days as an engine stoker when he was roasted down his front and chilled by icy draughts in the back.

His golf suffered along with his health and the titles grew scarcer, although he did manage to win two P.G.A. Match-Play Championships in the early sixties to set alongside the 1957 Dunlop Masters.

Brown held professional posts at Northumberland, Haggs Castle, Sandy Lodge,

Hartsbourne, Buchanan Castle and Cruden Bay before reducing his tournament commitments in 1968 to become pro to the Edinburgh Corporation courses.

A year earlier he had suffered a suspected heart attack and a stroke in 1976 cost him, temporarily, the power of speech and resulted in slight paralysis on one side of his body.

Always in conflict with authority, he resigned from the P.G.A. in 1974 — four years after being made captain of the Association — and soon after went into the licensed trade, running his own pub close to his beloved Hearts.

Around that time, Joan Brown began to require kidney dialysis treatment and Eric nursed her for six years before a successful transplant operation. She observed: 'I will always be sad that, as my health improved, Eric's deteriorated. He became introverted and couldn't play golf at all'.

Eric Brown may not have been everyone's idea of a favourite dinner guest, but he was impossible to ignore. He didn't win an Open, but laid claim to being Britain's top match-play golfer of his day. He certainly was 'A hell of a man'.

CAREER RECORD

OVERSEAS TITLES: Swiss Open 1951; Italian Open 1952; Irish Open 1953; Portuguese Open 1953.

DOMESTIC TITLES: Penfold Tournament 1952; Stuart C. Godwin 5000 Guineas 1956 (jt); Dunlop Masters 1957; *Yorkshire Evening News* Tournament 1958 (jt); P.G.A. Match-Play 1960-62; Dunlop Tournament 1960; Northern Open 1950-53-54-55-57; Scottish Professional Championship 1956-57-58-60-62-65-66 (jt)-68; Gleneagles Saxone Tournament 1957.

INTERNATIONAL: Ryder Cup 1953-55-57-59; Scotland in World Cup 1954-55-56-57-58-59-60-61-62-65-66-67-68; Scotland in Double Diamond 1971-72-73.

AMATEUR: Scottish Amateur 1946.

MISC: Harry Vardon Trophy 1957; Ryder Cup non-playing captain 1969-71; P.G.A. captain 1970.

7
TONY JACKLIN

SOME of the most spectacular triumphs have been plotted in the strangest of places. In Tony Jacklin's case, the improbable setting was a crowded dining room in one of Southport's most fashionable hotels.

The year was 1983 and Jacklin, the golfer who conquered the Americans at home and abroad between 1968 and '72, had barely three months to devise a strategy for his first taste of Ryder Cup captaincy that autumn.

Already he had won his first significant battle — to remove the stigma of 'second class citizens' which for years had lingered over the European team like a foul odour.

Now came the difficult part. Somehow, he had to convince Severiano Ballesteros that he was not only wanted, but was actually the pivotal player in Jacklin's Ryder Cup blueprint.

'I remember the moment clearly,' recalled Tony, who like Ballesteros had been omitted from the 1981 Ryder Cup side under controversial circumstances.

'I joined Seve for breakfast in the Prince of Wales Hotel during the 1983 Open at Birkdale. I knew I simply had to convince him that we all needed him and I also knew it was not going to be easy.'

Both men had been overlooked by a three-man selection committee for the '81 match at Walton Heath and, like a pair of recalcitrant children, both had decided to divorce themselves from future Ryder Cup activity.

Jacklin was first to recognise that there was no sense in harbouring grudges against the P.G.A; Ballesteros, with his fiery Latin temperament, was always likely to be a tougher proposition.

'I thought I was mad over what I saw as an injustice,' smiled Jacklin. 'But Seve . . . ! His reaction at that time towards playing in the Ryder Cup was "No way. Never!"

'Anyway, the Ryder Cup was just a few months away so as Seve's eggs grew colder, I tried to make my point.

'I said to him: "Seve, just listen to me. You're younger and you get more angry but if you think about it, your career is going to go a long way into the future — but not as long as the Ryder Cup. Think about that".'

Ballesteros, a man not kindly disposed towards compromise, shrugged expansively and at last offered Jacklin a glimmer of hope. 'I don't know. I'll see. Maybe!' he replied cautiously.

The breakfast time showdown ended without any positive indication that Ballesteros would climb down. However, Jacklin added: 'Then, of course, later in the week he came round, said "Okay" and that was that. I had the main man. Once you get a guy like Seve on your side, who is so respected by all the other players, everything falls into place.'

And the rest, as they say, is history. That particular Ryder Cup in Florida, with Jacklin at the helm and Ballesteros as his first lieutenant, narrowly failed to yield the coveted first victory on American soil.

But the one-point defeat allowed Jacklin and others a glimpse into the future: a vision that the golden prize would finally be captured by Europeans on American soil; a dream that was to become a reality at Muirfield Village, Ohio, in 1987.

By now Jacklin's captaincy was in its third term of office. The mistakes of the past had been banished, the close call at Palm Beach had been turned into an exhilarating victory at The Belfry in 1985 and the moment was ripe for Europe's inaugural triumph on American turf.

This time there were no mistakes as the Europeans mauled the team captained by The Golden Bear, Jack Nicklaus, on the course he designed and cultivated with such tender loving care.

Few people can forget the moving sight of Tony Jacklin, the first victorious captain of a European team in America, microphone thrust under his nose, breaking down in tears, voice choked with emotion.

Fewer still can fully understand just why Jacklin cracked in full view of the prying television camera. This, after all, was someone who handled the media circus with aplomb and poise after winning the British Open at Royal Lytham in 1969 and the U.S. Open at Hazeltine the following year. No tears of joy there.

Only Jacklin appreciated the implications of that famous victory at Muirfield Village. It was an outpouring of emotion born of years of frustration, rejection and loneliness in the United States.

Tony explained: 'It was a build-up of emotion. Part of it was because I had recollections of so many defeats in Ryder Cup competition and the fact that for so long I was the "lone ranger" as far as Europeans were concerned on the American tour.

'When I set out to play in America in '67, I was the only one from over here, and it wasn't easy. It wasn't easy listening to all their bullshit week in week out, but you just had to get on with it.

'There were all the trips, back and forth, and having no option but to bow down to their superiority for so long. America was such a grind, a wrench. Week in week out of bloody obscure motels, not knowing anybody, no galleries, no-one recognising that you existed. It was all Palmer and Nicklaus and you were making up the numbers.

'Well, I suppose all these things were pent up over the years and the elation, the thrill of breaking through that — I mean not just denting it, but going right through it, smashing it — was something only I could feel because I know what I went through.'

The triumph in America, when it finally arrived after 60 years of failure, proved conclusively that the balance of golfing power had veered towards this side of the Atlantic and Jacklin savoured it more than most.

He said: 'When I first went to the States some guys were so small-minded. If you won a tournament they would never acknowledge it, or if they did, they would say you were lucky. But, you know, when you were as motivated as I was, that just made me more determined.

'The fact that they (the Americans) get so annoyed makes it more fun. As long as they won't let their rules bend to players like Seve, while these rules persist, we will keep getting pleasure out of it. It might sound like a perverse pleasure but that's how it is!'

Luckily for Jacklin, the majority of golfers who comprised his Ryder Cup teams shared those feelings, including the once-reluctant Ballesteros who is now one of the competition's staunchest supporters.

Yet neither the breathtaking achievements nor the euphoric climax to the '87 Ryder Cup would have been possible had Jacklin not performed a complete somersault when Ken Schofield, Executive Director of the P.G.A. European Tour, casually enquired if he might consider the captaincy in '83.

'I was in a state of shock,' recalled Tony. 'I mean, 1981 had been such a fiasco. I couldn't believe it when Mark James was chosen ahead of me, and leaving out Seve, the best player in the world, was ridiculous. It was just too ridiculous to talk about, if you really wanted to win the Cup.

'You can't ignore the best player in the world just because his manager got everybody's backs up over appearance money or whatever the issue was at the time. I mean it was stupid.

'I was invited to go to Walton Heath in an official capacity but I just told them to go and stick it in their ear. I didn't want to know and, as far as I was concerned, that was it. The Ryder Cup and I were divorced!'

However, time heals and when Schofield tested the water in the spring of 1983, Jacklin relented. He admitted: 'I thought, well, vendettas are a bit pointless and in any case the Ryder Cup and the European tour will be around long after I'm gone.

'I had to decide whether I wanted to do it. I thought if I was going to swallow my pride I was damned if I was going to do the job on the basis that I'd been involved in the past as a player. It had to be first-class.

'I mean, how can you hope to compete if you don't have the same resources? You can't expect guys who are perfectionists in their field to be comfortable in the back of the bus. That was crystal clear to me.

'We were fidgeting about for years, wondering who paid for what. Did the P.G.A.

pick up the tab for drinks? Was dry-cleaning included on the bill? Could you take along a girlfriend if you weren't married? All these petty issues were to the fore. Crazy!'

Jacklin weighed up all those factors and went to face the P.G.A. with his demands. He said: 'I told them we had to go by Concorde. They replied "Fine", so I said "All right, I'll take the job".'

After intimating his acceptance in May 1983, Tony busied himself with the minutiae which had been overlooked in the past, and finally the European team flew to Florida — by Concorde, of course — and to the P.G.A. National Golf Club at Palm Beach Gardens.

If there had been any doubts over Jacklin's commitment or capabilities, the 1983 Ryder Cup dispelled both. He quickly proved himself to be an astute, clear-thinking captain who was neither afraid nor slow to take a chance.

The inspired pairing of Ballesteros and the youthful Paul Way yielded two and a half points out of four. The combination of Faldo and Langer brought three out of four. But Jacklin delivered his *coup de grâce* on the eve of the last day.

Europe had edged into a narrow lead after the opening day but the match was poised on a knife edge at 8-8 with only the 12 singles remaining.

Traditionally, in the Ryder Cup, the best players were reserved to last . . . but Jacklin's shrewd ploy to break with that tradition very nearly won the match for the Europeans.

'That's the way it was in the old days. Jack Nicklaus and I played each other twice at Birkdale in 1969 and we were last out both times. I reckoned, this is not an exhibition match, it's the Ryder Cup, so let's try something different.

'In 1983 I figured, "What's the use of putting the power at the end if you've lost the match? Let's try to get some points on the board to give others confidence. Let's get Seve up top and put some reliable anchor men near the end".'

Tony's eyes twinkled — like a mischievous schoolboy who had played a prank on a pal — as he related how Nicklaus, the American captain, reacted. 'When the envelopes were opened, Jack's eyes almost popped out of his head. He spluttered and blurted out: "How could you do that?" It obviously never occurred to him to do that. Personally, I feel you must try everything possible, in the fairest sense, to win.'

The gamble almost paid off as Ballesteros halved while Faldo and Langer, playing at No 2 and No 3, both won. Unfortunately others simply 'didn't come through in the end', as Jacklin put it succinctly.

'Gordon Brand and Jose Maria Canizares both came up the 18th and it looked as if they would do it. But both played the hole indifferently which you can do under pressure. God, we all know that — we saw the Americans do it at Muirfield Village. We're all human.'

Brand lost by two holes to Bob Gilder; Canizares — at one stage three up — halved with Wadkins who conjured up a glorious 70-yard wedge to 15 inches on the last. Who could blame Nicklaus for planting a mock kiss on the divot which Wadkins' wonder shot had torn up?

Nicklaus's relief was nowhere near as great as Jacklin's disappointment. America had retained the Cup by a single point, and the European captain was inconsolable. 'That was as big a disappointment as not winning the 1972 Open at Muirfield,' confessed Tony. 'I've never felt as low as I was when we didn't win that Ryder Cup.

'I think I was more shocked, more numbed, when Trevino chipped in at Muirfield, but in that Ryder Cup it was just sheer, abject disappointment. Not in the performance of the lads, but from the fact that I couldn't help feeling we were going to win because we were ahead for most of that last afternoon. Then two games switched things round and they got their noses in front.'

Defeat, yes, but defeatist . . . never. The two years between Palm Beach and The Belfry 'whizzed past' according to Tony, who used to see Ballesteros and a few others intermittently, and the subject was always the same: 'We'll get them next time'. They were right.

The 15th of September, 1985, will long be remembered as the day Europe won the Ryder Cup for the first time in 28 years, and by the comprehensive margin of $16\frac{1}{2}$-$11\frac{1}{2}$.

Yet the week began badly, with Lee Trevino's team establishing a 3-1 lead from the opening foursomes, before a second-day fightback carried Europe into a 9-7 lead going into the singles. Again Jacklin outfoxed his rival.

'We had a little chat about the singles order in the team room and I said: "Strength in the middle this time". That provoked a debate so I left the room, got out a notepad and pen and wrote down the names as they came into my head — Pinero, Woosnam, Way, Ballesteros, Lyle, Langer, Torrance, Clark, Rivero, Faldo, Canizares, Brown.

'I went back into the room and told them that was how we were going to do it. Manuel Pinero leapt a foot into the air because he was so delighted at getting Wadkins.'

Pinero beat Wadkins, Paul Way stunned Ray Floyd, and from that moment Jacklin scented victory. The powerful middle order of Ballesteros, Lyle and Langer delivered two and a half points and ultimately Sam Torrance claimed the honour of sinking the winning birdie putt against Andy North on the 18th, pencil still behind one ear and both arms raised aloft in a two-fisted salute.

'That was pure theatre,' recalled Jacklin with obvious pride. 'It was like it was meant to be that way, when Howard Clark's putt at the 17th lipped out leaving Sam to finish the business. European golf came of age at that moment and I shall remember it for the rest of my life.

'The whole week's tension and anxiety was swept away, the pent-up emotion released. It was just sheer, uncontrolled euphoria.'

And so to Muirfield Village, the course that Jack built, in Nicklaus's home town of Columbus, Ohio. By now, only the Americans themselves doubted whether Europe could cross new frontiers and win the Ryder Cup in the United States. They were in for a rude awakening.

Once again, Jacklin's preparations had been meticulous, and the fact that America's non-playing captain, Nicklaus, was certain to 'trick up' Muirfield to suit his team only heightened the sense of anticipation.

From the moment he marched down the steps of Concorde, Jacklin left the Americans in no doubt of his intentions. In the verbal sparring, Tony's aggressive jabs scored more points than Jack's defensive responses.

However, Jacklin's declaration: 'We're here to win for the first time on American soil' began to sound like an idle boast on the opening morning. Torrance and Clark lost to Curtis Strange and Tom Kite by 4 and 2; Ken Brown and Langer fell 2 and 1 to Hal Sutton and Dan Pohl. Further behind on the course, Faldo and Woosnam trailed Wadkins and Larry Mize by four holes at the turn and Ballesteros and young Jose Maria Olazabal were two down after six to Larry Nelson and Payne Stewart.

The cherished dream was in danger of vanishing on the first morning, but Jacklin was unconcerned. 'Sure, we didn't have it all our own way but what do you do? We were keyed up and we had prepared the best we knew how. You can practise all you like and still get on the first tee and have a double bogey then wonder if you've blown your chances already. I think that was how we felt that morning. However, nothing wakes you up like a double bogey!

'But, this time, we were confident deep down because we had won in '85. There was a deep-rooted belief that we could actually do it and that was the reason we were able to recover. The clean sweep in the afternoon emphasised that point.'

As Jacklin watched, his players worked at trying to extricate themselves from a genuine crisis. Faldo and Woosnam won six of the last nine holes to ignite the recovery while Ballesteros and Olazabal also wrung a vital point from a potential defeat.

Then for the first time in Ryder Cup history, Europe whitewashed an American team in one session, grabbing all four points in the fourballs for a 6-2 lead at the end of the first day.

That four-point lead became five after a spellbinding second day, particularly the afternoon fourballs where the two teams reeled in 87 birdies and two eagles. Jacklin called it 'pure, unadulterated inspiration'.

Needing just four points out of 12, Tony's last-day strategy involved placing his big guns in the middle-lower order. But little did he think that the most valuable contribution would come from Irishman Eamonn D'Arcy, who sank a teasing four-foot downhill putt on the last to edge out Ben Crenshaw.

Eight of the dozen singles went to that 18th hole and as Jacklin pointed out: 'Down the closing stretch, we were tougher than the Americans. Not one of our lads lost the 18th. So often in the past it was the other way round.

'That is what the game of golf, in essence, is all about. The confidence to go through with your feelings. It's all in the head at that level.'

When Langer halved with Nelson, the match was safe. Soon after, Ballesteros —

who else? — beat Curtis Strange 2 and 1. Europe had won. Ballesteros and Jacklin embraced.

Twice, American interviewer Ed Sneed attempted to elicit a comment from Jacklin but was confronted by tears. He tried twice more but finally settled for a mumbled: 'It has been the greatest day of my life' from the victorious captain.

Considering the same man had won two 'major' championships, it was a remarkable admission, but nowadays Jacklin is able to put his Open titles and Ryder Cup triumphs into a proper perspective.

'I felt great personal pride in winning the British and U.S. Opens; being captain of the Ryder Cup wins was a different sensation. It's almost like moving on from being an actor to a director, if you know what I mean.

'When you're young, you just want to act, then as you get older you become a director. Both have ways of providing satisfaction, but I feel the significance of the Ryder Cup victories is far greater than individual performances.

'As an individual, you can only experience so much emotion. When you're involved with a team, it's a pretty awesome thing. The Opens were for the benefit of Tony Jacklin; the Ryder Cups were for the good of European golf.'

With apologies to Jacklin's own analogy, the eighties have seen him become golf's equivalent of Steven Spielberg, but in the sixties and seventies, he was undoubtedly British golf's answer to Harrison Ford. And even Indiana Jones would have found it difficult to follow his swashbuckling adventures on both sides of the Atlantic.

However, it was surprising that Tony became a golfer at all. He was born in industrial Scunthorpe on July 7th, 1944 and unlike several other golfers in this book, was not blessed with a parental grounding in the game.

He only took up golf by accident at the age of eight and did not even own a full set of clubs until becoming assistant professional to Bill Shankland at Potters Bar ten years later.

Success came quickly. Tony won £1408 and the Gor Ray Assistants Championship in 1965 and the following year met and married his first wife, Vivien, who died so tragically near the Jacklin family home in Sotogrande in 1988.

In 1967 Tony recorded the first televised hole in one at the 16th at Royal St. George's, *en route* to capturing the Dunlop Masters, and came a promising fifth in the British Open at Hoylake. But the following year convinced the ambitious young Englishman that greater goals awaited him.

'Of course I always wanted to win our Open, but the dream didn't become a reality until 1967 when I went to America and got my card there. I learned a lot from Tom Weiskopf, Bert Yancey and Tommy Bolt who taught me to use my legs properly.

'In Britain you could be playing in a hurricane at Birkdale or wherever and you had to compromise your swing. Improvise. You never got a chance to work on technique.

'But once I got that sorted out and was able to test it under pressure by winning the Jacksonville Open in 1968, I thought: "Christ, I've won a tournament in America. I must

Shake on it. Henry Cotton is congratulated on his victory in the 1948 Open Championship by the previous year's winner, Fred Daly.

Henry Cotton the golf course designer, pictured at Fraserburgh in the North-East of Scotland in 1971.

'The Maestro'. Henry Cotton at Sotogrande on Spain's Costa del Sol in 1976.

Henry Cotton, 78 years young but still enjoying the Royal and Ancient game, two years before his death in 1987.

Henry Cotton, three-times Open champion, pictured just a few months before his death in 1987.

Dai Rees

The breakthrough. Dai Rees, only 23, pictured before the first of his record four victories in the *News of the World* Match-Play Championship. Rees beat Ernest Whitcombe (right) in the final at Oxhey, Herts, before receiving his prize from Sir Emsley Carr (centre).

Fred Daly looking relaxed during the 1952 Open Championship at Royal Lytham.

'Let's shake on it.' Fred Daly does not appear too downcast after losing to Dai Rees in the semi-final of the *News of the World* Match-Play at Ganton in 1953. Rees lost to Max Faulkner in the final.

Two of the greats from either side of the Atlantic. Dai Rees and Ben Hogan toast each other with a glass of milk during the Welshman's visit to America just after the War.

Dai Rees loosening up at Royal Lytham and St. Annes.

Dai Rees accepts his trophy after capturing the P.G.A. Seniors title at Coventry in 1966.

The Faulkner follow-through. Max Faulkner driving off at the Daks Tournament at Royal Mid Surrey in 1950.

Is this really mine? Max Faulkner looks as if he cannot believe that he has fulfilled a lifetime's ambition by winning the Open at Royal Portrush in 1951.

Max Faulkner in action against Cary Middlecoff in the 1953 Ryder Cup at Wentworth. Note the hi-tech newsreel camera in the background.

Super Mex meets Super Max! Two former Open champions indulge in a spot of comedy at St. Andrews in 1970.

'Himself' in action. A youthful Christy O'Connor plays to the camera.

A slightly windswept look for Christy O'Connor.

Studying the line . . . Christy O'Connor at Royal Lytham in 1969, underlining the maxim that 'You're never too old'. Christy finished fifth behind Tony Jacklin at the age of 44.

Eric Brown

A study in concentration. Eric Brown follows the flight of the ball anxiously.

The 'Brown Bomber' in explosive action. Eric Brown unleashes another booming drive on his way to a famous Ryder Cup victory over Tommy Bolt at Lindrick. Britain and Ireland won the trophy for the first time in 24 years.

Eric Brown in contemplative mood after being named Ryder Cup Captain for a second term in 1971. Note the 1957 Dunlop Masters jacket beginning to look a little threadbare!

On his way to becoming one of Britain's post-war greats. Tony Jacklin in familiar pose during the 1968 Open Championship at Carnoustie. Twelve months later he would be champion.

Hmmm . . . what's the line here? Tony Jacklin deep in thought on the 17th at Royal Lytham en route to his Open championship success.

Have shoes will travel. Tony Jacklin is spoiled for choice . . . pity he remembered to bring only one club!

Nice to see you . . . to see you, nice! Bruce Forsyth adjusts his headgear before setting out on a round with newly-crowned U.S. Open Champion, Tony Jacklin, in 1970.

Get in the hole! Tony Jacklin willing his ball to drop during his historic head-to-head with Lee Trevino in the 1972 Open at Muirfield.

Royal Lytham 19 years on . . .Tony Jacklin keeps a careful eye on his tee shot at the first hole in the 1988 Open.

Only 20 years old, but a star in the making. Bernard Gallacher in the swing of things at Lytham in 1969.

Nice swing, shame about the trousers! Bernard Gallacher attempts to dazzle the opposition.

Bernard Gallacher follows the flight of the ball during the 1975 Open at Carnoustie.

A study in concentration . . . Bernard Gallacher winds himself up for another mighty swipe.

Some people have golf on the brain . . . Bernard Gallacher has it on his trousers!

Nick Faldo

A youthful Nick Faldo pictured during the European Open at Turnberry in 1979.

Nick Faldo seldom takes a back seat . . . he sits on top of it instead.

On his way to the Open title . . . Nick Faldo takes an iron for safety at Muirfield's first hole at the start of his third round.

'It's all mine.' New Open champion Nick Faldo proudly displays the most celebrated trophy in golf after his 1987 win at Muirfield.

Nick Faldo lost in thought as he waits his turn to play.

Sandy Lyle

A few feet of rough never troubled anyone . . . at least not if you possess Sandy Lyle's enormous strength. Lyle on his way to capturing the European Open at Turnberry in 1979.

I belong to Glasgow. Sandy Lyle, who played for England as an amateur, signposts his wish to follow his father's Glaswegian roots at Haggs Castle in 1983.

Take one set of clubs, one remarkable golfer and what do you get? The famous silver claret jug in the middle! Sandy Lyle, with trophy, shortly after his 1985 Open Championship triumph.

If looks could kill. Sandy Lyle, suitably dressed for a typical summer's day at Turnberry, glowers at his ball after it stays out of the hole in the 1986 Open.

Sandy Lyle coaxes the ball into the hole during the Dunhill cup at St Andrews.

'Here, Dave, you hold onto my wallet and I'll earn some more cash for both of us.' Sandy Lyle and caddie Dave Musgrove in relaxed mood before the Bell's Scottish Open at glorious Gleneagles in 1988.

Reading the line . . . Sandy Lyle in action during the Bell's Scottish Open at Gleneagles.

Ian Woosnam

Ian Woosnam launches another iron off the tee during the 1987 Open at Muirfield.

The little man packs a mighty wallop . . . Ian Woosnam driving during the 1984 Open at St, Andrews.

Putting on the style. Ian Woosnam on his way to victory in the Bell's Scottish Open in 1987.

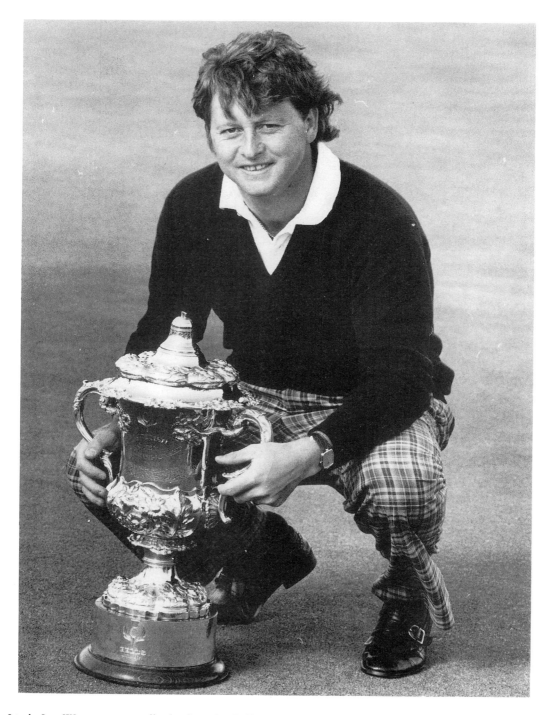

Little Ian Woosnam proudly displays the Bell's Scottish Open trophy he won in runaway fashion at Gleneagles.

Following the flight . . . Ian Woosnam during the 1987 Open at Muirfield.

The workman and his tools . . . Ian Woosnam prepares to set out on another round.

have a chance of winning the Open now".'

That same year Tony shot 80 in the last round of the Open at Carnoustie to finish 16th but he admitted: 'It was a question of learning to handle pressure. I knew then I was almost ready.'

In 1969, he became the first British golfer to win the Open since Max Faulkner in 1951 amid euphoric scenes at Royal Lytham. Yet he pointed out: '1969 was my worst year ever! But nobody remembers that. I won the Open but did nothing else. In fact, I went back to America the week after winning and failed to qualify four times in a row.'

Opening rounds of 68 and 70 left Jacklin three strokes behind left-hander Bob Charles, but a third-round 70, to the New Zealander's 75, altered the complexion of the championship. Jacklin headed the field by two strokes, and remained in that position after a closing 72 for a total of 280.

'Fortunately, no-one came in with a terrific last round,' he said with undue modesty. 'I actually played better at Muirfield than I did at Lytham and didn't win. But if you're there often enough, like Nicklaus, maybe you'll win a few.'

In truth, Jacklin could, with luck, have won three British Opens — including the infamous championship at Muirfield, of which we'll hear more later.

One year on after Lytham, Jacklin launched an imperious attack on St. Andrews and reached the turn in 29 shots in the first round. Then the heavens opened, Tony marked his ball in a bush and returned the next day to shoot a 67 when a 62 or 63 had seemed a realistic score.

'Circumstances took over. I felt so inspired that day. It was dream golf but what happened next was just one of those things. I don't look back and say I was unlucky at St. Andrews. As it turned out I still finished fifth and then missed out by only one shot at Birkdale the following year.'

However, a month before St. Andrews, Tony had captured the U.S. Open at Hazeltine National, Minnesota, and so became the first British winner of that title since Ted Ray in 1920.

Jacklin led from start to finish and won by seven strokes. He shot rounds of 71, 70, 70 to move two, three then four strokes clear of the field with one round to go.

'It was just one of those fantastic weeks. I putted incredibly well and no-one could wish for a better tournament. I established a lead on the first day and increased it every day.'

But Jacklin did face a crisis of confidence midway through his final round. He said: 'I missed a four-footer for a birdie at the seventh, then failed with a shorter one for par at the eighth. I still had a cushion, a good cushion, but suddenly the inward nine was looking like a long slog.

'At the ninth I hit this putt hard, far too hard, but it struck the back of the hole, jumped up and went in. I mean, it would have gone five feet, probably six feet past, and the way I was feeling I know I would have missed it.

'After that I holed a 15-footer for a birdie at the 10th and it was plain sailing again. Good fortune comes and goes in a round and you have to be mentally able to take advantage of the good breaks.'

Jacklin completed a closing 70 by sinking a 35-foot birdie putt with unerring accuracy at the 72nd hole to complete his seven-stroke success.

It was to be his last major title, and the reason for that came in the chunky, chuckling, larger-than-life figure of Lee Trevino. As Tony has inferred frequently since that fateful day, the dramatic events at Muirfield in 1972 broke his heart.

A second British Open title was in his grasp as he and Trevino reached the 71st hole sharing the lead. Unbelievably, Trevino chipped in from off the green for a par five. Jacklin three-putted for a six.

Ten minutes later Trevino parred the last and another dropped shot cost Tony second place. He stumbled off the green in a state of shock, a broken man.

'It was something I just never recovered from,' he said with admirable candour. 'Of course, I went on to win tournaments, but I was never again a threat in the majors. It was the watershed in my career.

'I was the best golfer at Muirfield. I know that without a shadow of a doubt. However, I've studied the old films and I still wince; it still shakes me up.'

Like a boxer who has taken one punch too many, Jacklin's nervous system appeared to blow a fuse and his career during the seventies went into decline as his putting touch vanished.

'I lost a lot of confidence in my putting in the mid-seventies and never really regained it,' he admitted. 'It became extra hard work. It became, at the end of the day, the only thing that made me unhappy. I never thought I'd live to see that day.

'Of course, I won the P.G.A. in 1982 and that was the last title. After that I more or less decided that enough was enough.'

Luckily, the Ryder Cup offer came along to fill the void, then the Jacklin family — already tax exiles in Jersey — uprooted and emigrated to Sotogrande in the balmy south of Spain.

'Success means that your privacy, your personal life, becomes different. I get left alone in Sotogrande and that suits me. I'm involved in the San Roque club which is under construction. It's going to be a great course.'

Tragedy struck the Jacklin household in 1988 when Vivien died suddenly. However, Tony insisted: 'I knew I had to stay here (in Sotogrande) after Vivien died. It was a damned remote and lonely place until I met Astrid, my wife now, but I was committed to this project from a financial standpoint. It was four years of my life and I couldn't walk away.'

As events at The Belfrey and Muirfield Village proved, Tony Jacklin, OBE, has never walked away from any challenge and the world of golf has surely not heard the last of the most successful Ryder Cup captain on this side of the water.

CAREER RECORD

MAJOR TITLES: British Open 1969; U.S. Open 1970.

OVERSEAS TITLES: Kimberley Tournament (South Africa) 1966 (jt); Forest Products Tournament (New Zealand) 1967; New Zealand P.G.A. 1967; Greater Jacksonville Open 1968-72; Lancome Trophy 1970; Dunlop International (Australia) 1972; Italian Open 1973; Bogota Open 1973; Los Lagartos Open 1974; Scandinavian Enterprises Open 1974; German Open 1979; Venezuelan Open 1979.

DOMESTIC TITLES: Blaxnit Tournament 1966; Pringle Tournament 1967; Dunlop Masters 1967-73; W.D. & H.O. Wills Open 1970; Benson and Hedges Festival 1971; Viyella P.G.A. 1972; Kerrygold International Classic 1976; English Professional 1977; Jersey Open 1981; Sun Alliance P.G.A. 1982.

INTERNATIONAL: Ryder Cup 1967-69-71-73-75-77-79; GB v Europe 1976; England in World Cup 1966-70-71-72; England in Double Diamond 1972-73-74-76-77.

MISC: Rookie of the Year 1963; Braid Taylor Memorial Medal (highest British placing in Open) 1969-70-71-72; Association of Golf Writers Trophy 1969-70; Tooting Bec Cup 1972 (jt); Ryder Cup captain 1983-85-87-89; Hon. Life President P.G.A.

8

BERNARD GALLACHER

FEW golfers embody the British bulldog spirit as effectively as Bernard Gallacher. The post-war era has produced better strikers of the ball, but it is doubtful if they were possessed with the almost demonic desire to win which has become the Gallacher trademark.

To the majority of recreational players, the golf course is a place to relax; to Bernard it is a battlefield where winning and losing are almost as important as life and death.

Lee Trevino, in his own inimitable style, once remarked that 'You gotta dance with what you brung', which was another colourful way of saying that you should make the best of your ability.

Bernard Gallacher has made a career out of doing precisely that and, like another son of Bathgate, Eric Brown, he has habitually produced his best when the stakes were large and his prospects alarmingly slim.

Whether he is fighting a slice or a hook, chipping badly or putting indifferently, Gallacher's combative nature can turn a potentially disastrous round into a satisfactory one.

Inevitably, the Ryder Cup was an ideal vehicle for Gallacher to develop a reputation as one of the most pugnacious, single-minded, toughest competitors in the history of the event.

The cut and thrust of games against the Americans stimulated Bernard's patriotic feelings and transformed him from an affable bloke off the course into a snarling adversary as soon as he arrived on the first tee.

'You've got to show your opponent that you mean business,' said Gallacher. 'You're not going out there for an exhibition match, you're going out to win and I always made certain that my opponents knew they were facing a really tough match.

'It's part of the psychology. Some recoil from it; others show they're equally determined to get stuck in. The Americans are quite tough and I think they respect someone who's going to play hard and not give in easily.'

The man who shaped that way of thinking was another typically tenacious battler, Brian Huggett, the little Welshman who captained the Great Britain and Ireland team in 1977.

'Brian was the person who really showed me what competing was all about. He has the most fantastic attitude, especially towards the Ryder Cup. Even if it looked as if he was about to lose, say, 4 and 3, he would fight like grim death to hang on and get beaten 3 and 2 or 2 and 1. That mattered to him and it matters to me.

'The Americans show a professional respect for that. I want to see all the putts in during Ryder Cup matches. My old pal Brian Barnes would happily concede three or four footers but not me! I refuse to give my opponent anything. I make it clear he has to win his matches!'

Apart from that reluctance to give anything away, Gallacher is utterly fearless. He admitted: 'I've never felt scared of anyone, no matter how big a name he might be. Maybe that's why I've always done quite well against them. When I turned professional I was apprehensive about how I played — not about the guys I was playing alongside.

'My yardstick has always been the same — only worry about getting the pars and the birdies. In match-play I've tried to eliminate playing the person and concentrated instead on playing the course. My attitude is simply: "It's me against the course".'

Bernard proved remarkably adept at winning his matches in that manner, as his Ryder Cup record verifies. In eight consecutive appearances he played 31 times — and only Neil Coles, Tony Jacklin and Christy O'Connor have surpassed that. But none of that trio can hold a candle to Gallacher's record of 13 wins, 13 defeats and 5 halves.

Of all the victories, carved out of sheer tenacity and a cocoon of concentration on the course, the one which still brings a faint smile to his face is the 1977 success over Jack Nicklaus. 'That match has to be the most satisfying,' he conceded. 'Jack Nicklaus, in the eyes of most pros, amateurs and even non-golfers, is the greatest player over the last 30 years. In a sense he was a guy you wanted to avoid, while another part of you fancied the chance of a shot at him.'

The luck of the draw determined that Gallacher had no say in that matter. He was scheduled to face The Golden Bear, at the height of his considerable powers, and for Bernie it represented a heaven-sent opportunity to forget the distress of being omitted from the Friday fourball series by Huggett.

'I remember the team performed poorly that year at Royal Lytham, which was the last before the continentals became involved. But the Americans were also exceptionally strong and we had virtually lost the match before the 10 singles on the last day.

'Anyway, it's fair to say that it was more difficult than normal to try to play the course that afternoon! I suppose that was inevitable against Jack but I tried to stick to my normal plan and my thoughts were focused on getting a par at the first.'

But before the match could even begin, Gallacher had another problem to surmount when his treasured Golden Goose putter was stolen minutes before the players were called to the tee.

'I was using it on the practice putting green before my game, but somebody "nicked" it between there and the first tee. Goodness knows how it happened but the club never turned up again.

'At that time I wasn't putting especially well so I reckoned the change wouldn't do any harm. I thought it might be a good excuse if I lost to Jack!'

The loss of possibly the most important club in the bag might have reduced most mortals to a state of apoplectic rage. Bernard simply bought himself a new Ping putter instead.

'Once we got started I went 3, 4, 4, 3 — one under par — to go four up. I suppose I was a little startled to find myself in that position but I also played the fifth well and almost won it while Jack really had to scramble for his half at the sixth.'

There was an air of predictability about what happened next. 'I wasn't jumpy at finding myself four up after four, but I became less attack-minded. I started to protect my lead and, of course, you can't do that against a player like Jack Nicklaus.

'You've got to go out there and attack the course the whole way round. I became more defensive while Jack started to put it all together and he just wore me down.'

Slowly but surely Nicklaus clawed his way back into the tie and rammed in an 18-foot putt for a birdie 3 at the 16th to square the match. Now the Bear had his quarry firmly in his sights and prepared to move in for the kill.

However, the idea of defeat never occurred to a dogged fighter like Gallacher. Lytham's 17th hole is notoriously tough in normal circumstances, but all square with Jack Nicklaus and two to play was anything but normal.

'Amazingly, I still wasn't worried,' insisted Bernie. 'I felt I should have won the match, but knew we had everything to play for.'

Gallacher found the putting surface in two regulation blows, but faced an awkward putt of 85 feet for a birdie. The new Ping did its job, or more precisely its owner did, and Bernard sunk to his knees in sheer delight when the ball disappeared.

'Even then I knew I wasn't home and dry so I forced myself to concentrate hard at the last. My second shot hung left and landed off to the left while Jack went through the green but pitched back stone dead. The pressure was really on me now.

'My ball was roughly where Seve Ballesteros's finished at the last hole in the 1988 Open — only he had all the green in the world to work with. Back in '77 the pin was only eight feet onto the green. I hit it into the little bank in front of me and thought I caught it well.

'However, it ran past about five feet and somehow I holed it to beat the great man. That must go down as a truly memorable moment in my career.'

That same career has been studded with countless other memorable moments, both in the Ryder Cup and in medal play tournaments in which Gallacher demonstrated the same ruthless qualities that were evident against Nicklaus.

But as a youngster growing up in the town of Bathgate, he showed a precocious talent for golf and football. In fact his ability on the soccer pitch could have taken him to Easter

Road, home of his great passion — Hibernian Football Club. 'The ironic thing is that the Hibs scouts thought I was a cracking left back — when in fact I was a right half,' recalled Bernard.

'I remember playing for my school, St. Mary's Academy in Bathgate, and I was switched to left back because our regular No 3, a schoolboy international, was injured.

'I was only filling in but I played a "blinder" against an opponent who was right winger for the Scottish schools. After the match the scouts asked my teacher if I could go on trial at Easter Road but he replied: "Who, Bernard? He's a golfer, not a footballer".

'He was right, of course. Although football had been my first love at the age of 10 or 11, by the time I reached my mid-teens I was basically playing football just to keep fit. I certainly enjoyed the game and I'm still interested in it.'

That unswerving devotion to Hibernian served as a means of cutting the unbearable tension some years later, as Gallacher prepared to embark on a sudden-death play-off with Gary Player for the Dunlop Masters title at St. Pierre. Between his final round and the play-off, Bernard took time to find out how his beloved green and white heroes were faring against Dundee at Dens Park.

'Like myself,' he observed dryly, 'the Hibs are still drawing!' Then it was back to business, and a birdie 3 at the first extra hole was sufficient to beat Player for the 1974 championship.

But returning to Gallacher's adolescence, it was soon apparent that the small-framed but well-muscled youngster would embark on a golfing career.

He represented the British Boys team in 1965 at the tender age of 16 and within two seasons had established himself as one of Scotland's top amateur players in a particularly hard school.

The amateur scene at the time was dominated by Ronnie Shade, who won five consecutive Scottish titles, and Charlie Green, who was still winning national championships in his fifties.

'I had been playing against these guys since I was 15 and they taught me a thing or two. If you could keep up with them you could keep up with anybody.

'I used to play "Shadey" in the east and often ran up against Charlie through in the west. That helped me enormously. It toughened me up for my professional career ahead.'

The seasoned campaigners may have regarded Gallacher as something of an impudent young upstart, but he quickly showed that lurking beneath his cherubic, choirboy looks was a mean, unrelenting competitor.

In 1967, just a few months after his 18th birthday, Gallacher romped away with the inaugural Scottish open amateur stroke-play championship at Muirfield. His opening round of 66 constituted an amateur record at the time and the teenager simply sprinted clear of his field, winning by five strokes from Green and by six from Shade — even allowing himself the luxury of a closing 78.

It was in that final round that Gallacher first gave notice of his astonishing propensity for overcoming the odds. Despite a six-shot lead, he ran up a triple-bogey at the short fourth and turned in 40. Bets were being struck in the clubhouse about whether the cheeky boy would break 85, but Bernard shut a few mouths by strolling home in 38 to scoop the title.

Just when Walker Cup honours seemed a near certainty, Gallacher decided to turn professional, showing not for the last time that he was his own man. The decision taken, he set about rewriting the record books with an undisguised zeal.

In his first year as a professional Gallacher finished 32nd in the Order of Merit, offering a hint of things to come by finishing second to Peter Townsend in the Coca-Cola Young Professionals Championship at Coventry. He won £1200 in prizemoney in that debut season and Henry Cotton quickly seized on the young fellow's potential by naming him 'Rookie of the Year'.

Around that time he fell in with 1951 Open champion Max Faulkner, with whom he shared the same manager. It seemed an unlikely liaison, the eccentric extrovert Max and the canny 19-year-old Bernie — but that brief spell under Faulkner's tutelage was to prove a rewarding experience.

Max, who still regards Gallacher like a favourite nephew, admitted the ambitious young pro needed the rough edges smoothed out. He said: 'I can remember one exhibition match at Brighton and Bernard was just a young fellow.

'He came to me before we started and said: "I've lost my game, lost it completely. Can you help?" When I took a look I was heartbroken. I've seldom seen a club swung so badly. He had a steep swing and could hardly hit the ball. It looked awful!

'I took him aside and said: "Now look, if you don't get back to that wide backswing you're finished. If you keep swinging like that you can give the game up because you'll never be much cop the way you're swinging. It's gone to pieces".

'Well, he really took the advice to heart and turned wider and wider and started hitting the ball a treat in no time. Thankfully he's never lost it again and his putting was always wonderful. He's one of the best, Bernard. Definitely someone I would want on my side.'

Gallacher acknowledged the debt he owes that wise old owl. He confessed: 'Max was my coach and my inspiration for a couple of years between 1968 and '70. He showed me the professional ropes; how to play different shots, how to keep my spirits up when times were bad, how to handle it when things were good.

'I mean, he was the biggest influence on my career. Apart from being a wonderful swinger of the club he taught me how to cope with the stresses of being a professional golfer.'

Faulkner's style of course management also rubbed off on the impressionable youngster. 'It was Max who made me score well even if I was playing badly. That is what being a professional golfer is all about.

'Everybody can score well if you hit greens in regulation. It's the days when things go wrong that you need to work hardest. That means being defensive at certain holes, or playing to your strengths. I've always had a reasonable short game so I wouldn't take chances at big par fives.

'I'd lay up short, pitch on and take my luck with the putt. It's an attitude. I would never chuck in the towel even if I wasn't playing particularly well. In fact I won quite a few tournaments that way.'

Two perfect illustrations of that stubborn refusal to admit defeat came in major professional tournaments early in his career, the 1971 Martini International at Royal Norwich and the 1974 Carrolls International (now the Irish Open) at Woodbrook.

In the former, Bernard opened with a horrendous 80, eight over par. Few golfers, if indeed any, would have considered victory as a more likely alternative to missing the halfway cut. Gallacher, however, charged on like a boxer who doesn't know when to lie down.

In the subsequent three rounds he squeezed 15 birdies and an eagle from the East Anglian course, bogied just three holes, and strung together rounds of 67, 68 and 67 to claim the title and £1250 first prize by a shot from Kel Nagle.

The '74 experience was almost as sensational. Bernard takes up the story: 'I had been going along nicely in that tournament at Woodbrook — until the first hole of the last round.

'I ran up a three over par 8 and thought I had blown my chance. At that point I decided to attack and everything came off. I was nine under par for the rest of the round and my 68 was enough to beat Jack Newton by three strokes! It was one of the most outstanding 17 holes of golf I've played.'

However, 1969 was the year when Bernard Gallacher emerged as a truly potent force in European golf, culminating in his becoming the youngest British or Irish player to play in the Ryder Cup at 20 years, seven months, nine days.

The year began well . . . and continued in the same vein. Bernard claimed his first professional victory, the Zambian Eagle Open in April, and followed that up by capturing the Cock o' the North event in that same country a week later.

Back in Britain, he took the Schweppes Tournament at Ashburnham in May and added the W.D. and H.O. Wills event at Moor Park to his burgeoning collection of titles. Now the Ryder Cup was a tantalising possibility.

In the event, Gallacher — who went on to win the coveted Harry Vardon Trophy as leader of the European Order of Merit — missed out on automatic selection by a mere half a point. The top six went to Royal Lytham by right . . . but at the time Bernie was seventh with 875.5 points, 0.5 behind his old buddy, Brian Barnes.

Team captain Eric Brown ensured that Bathgate was doubly represented in that 1969 Ryder Cup by picking Gallacher as one of his half-dozen choices to complete the line-up.

'I didn't set out in professional golf with the ambition of making the Ryder Cup team,' explained Bernard. 'I just wanted to do well and as it happened I had a particularly good 1969. Apart from winning a few tournaments I think I was runner-up three times.'

The prospect of grappling with virtual demigods such as Nicklaus, Casper, Floyd and Trevino might have intimidated some 20-year-olds, but fear was an alien word to Gallacher.

'I already had some first-hand experience of playing with American golfers. Just before the '69 Open an exhibition match was lined up for Trevino, Orville Moody and myself at Dalmahoy near Edinburgh.

'Trevino was the new guy on the scene, having won the 1968 U.S. Open while Moody was the reigning U.S. Open champion. Funnily enough they didn't concern me in the slightest. I was never scared of these players — and I was never scared of winning. You're either born with it or you're not. It's inside you, it can't be taught.'

Gallacher raced round Dalmahoy in a five under par 67 to beat Trevino by five strokes and Moody by 11. 'One of the finest young players I have seen in my life' was Trevino's generous verdict.

'Trevino didn't intimidate me in any way. He talks all the time, he simply can't shut up, but I didn't let it worry me. Some golfers like Neil Coles didn't enjoy playing with him because he upset their concentration but he doesn't do it to put you off. He isn't devious in that respect. It's just the way he is.'

Gallacher and 'Supermex' were to cross swords six times in Ryder Cup foursomes, fourballs and singles — with the Scot emerging with the kudos after four wins, a half and one defeat.

Two of those points were obtained at Lytham in the famous halved Ryder Cup match, including a 4 and 3 singles success on the final afternoon as Britain and Ireland came agonisingly close to repeating their 1957 victory.

Other moments which Gallacher remembers with pride were the 1971 and '79 Ryder Cups in America. At St. Louis in '71, Bernard produced the best British record of three and a half points out of five and surpassed that at the Greenbrier eight years later by winning four matches out of five.

In three Ryder Cup appearances between '71 and '79 Gallacher was unbeaten in five singles in America, but surrendered that tag to the redoubtable Tom Watson at Palm Beach in 1983.

'That was one of my greatest disappointments,' he conceded. 'The week had gone badly because I lay in bed with flu and I felt rotten. I was last man out and although I went two or three down I didn't feel any pressure because the scoreboards indicated that we were going to win.

'Anyway, as it became apparent that our match was vital, I got the feeling that Watson was starting to wilt and I became inspired by his mistakes. Eventually I won the 16th to get back to one down.'

The 17th haunts Bernard still for, as he readily admits, he broke his own rules and played the man instead of the course. 'We both missed the green with our tee shots.

Watson's ball was sitting up perfectly but mine was lying badly. I mean you could hardly see it. Then I made the biggest mistake imaginable by guessing that Watson could make a three from his lie.

'It was a bad error because I tried to finesse this shot and, of course, the ball didn't come out. My next went four feet past while Watson hit an awful shot to 20 feet and missed. Even to this day I thought my four footer was perfect but it stayed out and I lost a wonderful chance to take him down the last. I was very disappointed.'

During the seventies, Gallacher formed the smaller half of a successful double act with Brian Barnes, a partnership which delivered 5½ points out of 10 in foursomes and fourball matches.

It seemed an unlikely combination: the cold, calculating Gallacher and the larger than life, cavalier Barnes. However, the pair dovetailed beautifully.

'I think our games complemented each other. He had a good long game and I had a good short game. However, Brian had a problem with his attitude. He was so laid back he could never take anything seriously and I had terrible trouble motivating him.

'My greatest problem was trying to keep him away from the beer tents! In America it was so hot Brian was always looking for a cold beer. I mean, I would never have dreamed of doing that but Brian was a law to himself.

'I had to keep one eye on our match and one eye on Barnsey. Still, he was such a good player I knew he would always come through because he had plenty of "bottle".'

Humour was also a vital ingredient in the partnership. Barnes smiled at the recollection of one moment during the 1973 Ryder Cup at Muirfield which epitomised Bernard's dry wit.

'A few of us were sitting in the dining room of our hotel in North Berwick enjoying breakfast and Billy Casper and his wife were at another table. Suddenly the swing doors burst open and in walked Bernie.

'He strolled past Casper's table and, without pausing, said loudly: "Good Mormon, Bill!" I think it took people a few seconds to appreciate the comment and the entire dining room dissolved in laughter.'

Bernard went on to finish in the top 10 in the Order of Merit on six occasions and at the start of the 1989 season had amassed £403,221 in official earnings to stand 25th in the all-time list of money winners.

The lucrative appointment as club professional at Wentworth following the death of his friend and mentor Tom Haliburton in 1975 forced him to divide his interests but he confounded the sceptics by combining both jobs successfully.

Gallacher continued to be a prolific winner in Europe, becoming the first and so far only player to defend the Dunlop Masters, lifting the Spanish and French Opens and winning the Haig Whisky T.P.C. event in 1980 to secure a place in the World Match-Play at his home course of Wentworth, where he eventually finished third.

The only serious blot on a spectacular career came in 'the big one', the British Open.

If his attitude to playing Ryder Cup was faultless, his approach to the Open was flawed.

'I've always disliked seaside golf as the element of luck seems to play a bigger part. I never got myself into a position to win it and that really disappoints me.

'There were times when I was going well and seemed to meet with some sort of disaster. I remember needing a 3, 4 finish at Troon in '73 for a 66 in the second round which would have pushed me into a challenging position. I ended up taking a six at the 17th and that was that.

'At Carnoustie in '75 I had a 67 in the second round but I've never managed to string good rounds together. It's an attitude problem. I've always seen golf as a game to be played through the air, even chip shots, which eliminate so much of the luck involved in pitch and run.'

Marriage to Lesley in 1973 has brought contentment and three youngsters, Kirsty, Jamie and the late arrival in 1987, Laura Kate. The elder pair are coming along nicely while Bernard runs a thriving shop with a staff of four assistants at Wentworth.

Nothing, however, can dull the competitiveness which has driven him throughout his career. Although he turned 40 at the start of 1989, the raw predatory instinct remains.

'I'll continue to practise hard, to play hard and who knows? I might still be winning tournaments years from now . . . and I would love to play in a winning Ryder Cup team.'

CAREER RECORD
OVERSEAS TITLES: Zambia Eagle Open 1969; Zambia Cock o' the North Tournament 1969; Mufulira Open (Zambia) 1970; Spanish Open 1977; French Open 1979.
DOMESTIC TITLES: Schweppes P.G.A. 1969; W.D. & H.O. Wills Open 1969; Martini International 1971-82;. Scottish P.G.A. 1971-73-74-77; Coca-Cola Young Professionals 1973; Carrolls International 1974; Dunlop Masters 1974-75; Haig Whisky T.P.C. 1980; Cold Shield Greater Manchester Open 1981; Jersey Open 1982-84.
INTERNATIONAL (Pro.): Ryder Cup 1969-71-73-75-77-79-81-83; Scotland in World Cup 1969-71-74-82-83; Scotland in Double Diamond 1971-72-73-74-75-76-77; Hennessy-Cognac Cup 1974-78-82-84.
AMATEUR: Scottish Open Amateur Stroke-Play 1967.
INTERNATIONAL (Amateur): British Boys 1965-66; Scotland in Home Internationals 1967.
MISC: Rookie of the Year 1968; Harry Vardon Trophy 1969; Scottish Sportsman of the Year 1969; Tooting Bec Cup (jt) 1975.

9
NICK FALDO

NICK Faldo sat alone with his thoughts as just 300 yards away his arch rival and Wentworth neighbour Sandy Lyle threw a party to celebrate victory in the Open Championship at Royal St. George's.

That summer of 1985 was the nadir of Faldo's professional career. The blue-eyed boy of English golf had never been at a lower ebb. His marriage had crumbled, his swing had been remodelled but, worst of all, his most bitter adversary had won a major title.

The golden days of 1983, when Nick performed like a latter-day King Midas, had become distant memories. From first place in the European Order of Merit that season with winnings of £140,761 he was on the slide towards an eventual 42nd position in 1985 with £30,140.

Since winning the Sea Pines Heritage Classic in South Carolina and the Car Care Plan International at Moortown in the spring of 1984, the flow of titles had dried up. The critics were sniping at his decision to construct a brand-new swing. But, deep down, Faldo retained an unshakable faith in himself and his mentor, David Leadbetter.

As he thought of Lyle enjoying the fruits of an Open triumph, Faldo became a man possessed. He recalled: 'It was the hardest moment of all to take. I just knew that I was good enough to win an Open myself. But at the time I was trying to rebuild my swing . . . and no-one else believed I could do it.

'I was going backwards as fast as Sandy was going forwards. I just looked at the pictures of Sandy, with the trophy and thought: "Right, you can do it too, so go out and prove it".

'I've been asked if Sandy Lyle's win in the Open at St. George's hadn't taken the pressure off me and the other British players. But the funny thing is that it seemed to make it worse. After he'd done that I wanted to prove myself to be an equal golfer.

'He's got a great record and I wanted to have one just the same. We all want to prove we're as good as all the others.'

Four years later Faldo not only proved he could win the Open Championship, but added a U.S. Masters title to his burgeoning collection and came agonisingly close to emulating Tony Jacklin's achievement of holding the British and American Open crowns simultaneously.

The slender young man from Welwyn Garden City in Hertfordshire had turned adversity into triumph, and the key lay in a bold decision to get back to basics.

Until 1984, the long, languid Faldo swing was aesthetically satisfying and, apparently, perfectly functional. It had served him well, particularly during the summer of '83 when Nick reaped a rich harvest from the European tour — five titles in total, including a record-equalling three in a row.

By the time of the '84 Open, Faldo was struggling to live up to the expectations of the British public and media. However, it still seemed reasonable to anticipate that his big breakthrough was just around the corner based on a sixth-place finish behind Seve Ballesteros at St. Andrews.

Faldo knew better. The following month he opened with a 69 in the U.S.P.G.A. at Shoal Creek and was handily placed until running up a reckless eight at the final hole of the second round. Another 'major' had slipped through his grasp on account of one or two slack shots.

It began to dawn on Nick that his rhythmic, free-flowing swing might not stand up to the sort of pressure which can only be found in the closing stages of a major championship.

Towards the end of the year, Faldo travelled to Sun City, Bophuthatswana in South Africa for the Million Dollar Challenge, plagued by self-doubt. There he met the man who not only changed his swing, but also his life.

'In the past I had chances to win the Open or get close to winning, but it never came off,' explained Faldo. 'At Birkdale in 1983 I had a good run and as far back as St. Andrews in 1978 I felt I had a chance. From that day on I believed I could win the Open.

'The trouble was that my game went off at the end of 1984 and the start of 1985. I wasn't happy around that time and I had no direction in my game. That's why I decided to go to David Leadbetter to seek his advice.'

Leadbetter, born in Surrey, raised in Zimbabwe and now a teaching pro in Florida, had established himself as something of a golfing guru. The pair, who had become acquainted at Sun City, met up again at Muirfield Village in Ohio during the spring of 1985, shortly after Faldo had failed by one shot to finish in the top 24 in the Masters and gain automatic entry into the following year's championship.

If Faldo had harboured reservations about his swing, Leadbetter brought them out into the open. 'Your swing is a thing of beauty, but it hides several fundamental flaws,' he told Nick.

Leadbetter concluded that the old swing would not stand up to last-round pressure and a radical rethink was essential if Faldo was to achieve his ultimate ambition and become Open champion. The attractive parts disguised the unsightly elements, he explained. The faults had to be eliminated . . . but it was going to take time.

The teacher told his willing pupil that it would need two years to complete the remodelling process. To an ambitious, young, successful professional golfer like Faldo, it was a supreme sacrifice.

'Two years for it all to work out is a hell of a long time. If I had known it was going to take that long I might have done it differently. I tried to change my swing while I was out on the Tour (in 1985), but had I known it was going to take so long I would have skipped a whole summer and gone to work with David for four months solid.

'I knew it was going to take a while because you have to gain confidence in any new method. With the old backswing I took the club inside and then my hands would go 'up' rather than remain on the same plane.

'As a result I got into the bad habit of having a flying right elbow. David taught me to flatten my left wrist position at the top of the backswing so that the right elbow tucked in much better. I started to achieve a better turn by remaining on the same plane.'

It was a long, difficult journey from Muirfield Village, Ohio in 1985 to Muirfield, Scotland in 1987. The trek took Faldo to the brink of despair. His obsession with perfecting the new swing resulted in sub-standard performances on the golf course. The deals dried up. His marriage was on the rocks.

But when Nick arrived at the East Lothian home of the Honourable Company of Edinburgh Golfers for the 116th Open Championship, he was ready to win. He insisted: 'I always believed that it was going to be my week.'

Leadbetter's prediction had been uncannily accurate. He had told Faldo that it would take two years to complete the transition and so it proved, although midway through the 1986 season Nick could at last see a chink of light at the end of a long, dark tunnel.

He had lost his playing privileges on the U.S. Tour, but the new method was definitely coming together, as a third place in the 1986 Whyte and Mackay P.G.A. and a fourth in the Peugeot French Open underlined. Fifth place in the British Open in foul conditions at Turnberry added to his growing conviction that the ordeal was almost over.

Nick finished the '86 season 15th in the Order of Merit with £71,138 and gained a new family when his second wife, Gill, gave birth to a daughter, Natalie. The omens for 1987 could scarcely have been healthier.

Following top-four finishes in both the Madrid and Italian Opens, Faldo won his first title for three years over the intimidating Las Brisas course on Spain's Costa del Sol. It was a course designed to separate the men from the boys and Nick eventually captured the Spanish Open with an aggregate of 286.

After a week's coaching from Leadbetter at the Bell's Scottish Open at Gleneagles, Faldo arrived at Muirfield full of optimism. It wasn't misplaced. Not only did the swing stand up to the pressure, it did so to such an extent that Nick dropped only five strokes to par over the 72 holes.

'In a way, my decision to change my swing was all geared up to what happened at Muirfield,' said Nick. 'It's not the great shots which win championships. It's the destructive ones which lose them. I had to eliminate them. I'm a perfectionist and I knew I had a lot of work to do before I could rely on my swing absolutely.'

Peter Oosterhuis, who partnered Faldo in three Ryder Cups, believes the change of swing supplied the final piece in the jigsaw. He said: 'Nick was always a good player but the swing change made him an exceptional one. It's untrue to say that I ever thought he would turn out quite as good but he was always very determined, a hard worker and patient. Patience is usually a virtue in golf and Nick has it in abundance.'

The portents were good when Faldo launched into the 1987 Open with three consecutive birdies, and after rounds of 68 and 69 he trailed American Paul Azinger by just one stroke. Scotland's notoriously unpredictable summer weather reserved its worst for those four July days, but Faldo sailed on serenely.

'Why isn't this championship held during the British summer?' demanded a cold, damp and miserable member of the Japanese press corps. Azinger, more used to equable conditions in the U.S.A., probably agreed with him.

After third-round 71s, on one of the most unpleasant golfing days imaginable, Azinger still held his single-shot advantage over Faldo and South African David Frost. Nick celebrated his 30th birthday that evening, then composed himself for the final push.

His closing round of 71 was memorable not for its flamboyance but for its astonishing consistency. Eighteen holes, eighteen pars. It sounds simple but it wasn't.

Azinger showed no signs of faltering by reaching the turn in 34 to increase his lead over Faldo to three shots. Nick missed birdie chances at the first five holes but made steady pars — before having to escape from sand three times in four holes from the seventh.

With two holes remaining, Azinger still led, although now by just one stroke, and Faldo's carefully rehearsed drills under pressure came into play. The Englishman gathered two more pars from the unforgiving course. Azinger collected two bogeys . . . and the title was Faldo's.

'It is the ultimate to play golf under these pressures. You want to be able to say that you were totally on top of it all and in complete control. I have always enjoyed meeting the demands that a golf course creates. To do so under pressure is even better.

'When I hit that five iron to the last at Muirfield in the final round I could hardly believe it. You stand up there and it all happens. You're working from memory. You're so nervous. It's similar to the feeling you have when you've almost had a car crash. You get that horrible shaky feeling and you go all hot and cold.'

But Faldo hadn't wilted. He proved he had the mental fortitude and the right method to win a 'major'. He admitted: 'For the last six holes I knew that one mistake could cost me the title and those holes are pretty tough. The whole idea of going to David (Leadbetter) was to build a swing which could cope with that.

'Winning the Spanish Open was important. It was a very similar win to Muirfield. I played well but didn't make all that many birdies. I played well to wear the other guys out.

'I honestly don't remember even scoring 18 consecutive pars in a single round . . . certainly not in the final round of the Open Championship! Looking at my score it might appear that I was in a conservative frame of mind, but nothing could be further from the truth. Naturally I wanted to make birdies but I wasn't going to force it and do something stupid.

'I had a lot of putts which I could have got carried away over, but I wanted to make it easy for myself. I was trying to hole them but if I missed them I didn't want to make it too tough coming back. That would have been daft. Suicidal really.

'I never looked at the leader board at all on the way round. There was no point in putting extra pressure on me. I knew it was close and that Paul was playing well, but I played my own game. I figured that if I got a four up the last the Open might be mine — and it's a difficult thing coming up the last knowing that you might need a par to win the title.

'On the 18th I hit a good three wood and then I gave it a blast with a five iron from around 200 yards. I think I pushed my first putt a little but whatever I did I sent it about five feet past, leaving myself the sort of putt no-one wants on the final green. I said to myself that the line was just inside the right edge. I told myself just to hit it hard enough. I told myself I must not dribble it or else it would never go in. Fortunately it did and that was that.'

In that instant, the despair he felt two years previously vanished. Now it was Faldo's turn to hold the party. Now he could scan the newspapers to absorb the story of his triumph instead of Sandy Lyle's.

That story was one of joy and despair, a victory for mind over matter. Faldo never at any time lost sight of his objectives during the bleak, depressing days of 1985 and '86, even on the occasions when he began to question if the physical and mental anguish was justified. Each time he returned to the same conclusion: it was worth getting worse in order to get better!

It was obstinate dedication which carried him over the threshold from outstanding professional to champion golfer. In fact, the same type of application which took him into the sport in the first place 17 years earlier.

From the outset, Nick loved sport and the little boy from Welwyn Garden City excelled at swimming and cycling. He was the Herts under-11 freestyle and breaststroke champion over 110 yards but soon took up the challenge of cycling.

Before long that, too, was relegated to the background as Faldo embarked on a new pursuit. He discovered golf, thanks to the medium of television. Colour was still in its infancy but Nick's parents bought a brand new set in 1971 and the family tuned in to the U.S. Masters.

'I watched the Masters that night on television and it was so exciting that I was hooked right from the start. At that time in my life I was looking for something other than a team sport. I played a lot of cricket at that age but team sports never really appealed to me because you can do your best as an individual but still end up on the losing side.

'As soon as I saw the Masters and those pictures from Augusta I knew that golf was the game for me. I saw Jack Nicklaus play well and I wanted to be like him,' recalled Faldo, who was spellbound by the vivid images from Augusta National: the beauty of the scenery, the bravura of the principal characters.

Faldo's parents recognised his genuine determination to be a golfer and booked half a dozen lessons for their son at the club just down the road.

'I was almost 14, then during my Easter holidays I went to Ian Connelly, my local pro at Welwyn Garden City, who taught me the basics of the game. In the beginning I never went out on to the course. Instead I practised all I could. I remember well that I didn't play my first round of golf until July 18th (his 14th birthday). I scored in the high 70s but that was without counting the lost balls because I didn't know the rules.

'Within two years I had got my handicap down to plus one and I was totally besotted by the game, so much so that when it came to my exams I told my teacher that I wouldn't be able to concentrate on them because I wanted to play golf so much.'

Little did Faldo know at the time that Augusta National would play such an integral part in his elevation to the top of the golfing class fully 18 years after that fleeting glimpse of the course on television.

'At that time I had no inkling that one day I would go on to win the Masters on a course which I had grown to love when watching Jack Nicklaus. Augusta is one of my favourite courses and now it has become that little bit special to me,' he said after his breathtaking 1989 triumph.

Nick's amateur career was short but successful. During 1974 and '75, he represented England at boys, youths and senior level and plundered some of the most inviting items of silverware on offer.

Just eight days after his 18th birthday in 1975, Faldo became the youngest winner of the English Amateur Championship, beating David Eccleston 6 and 4 in the final at Royal Lytham and St. Anne's. The following month at Pannal, he captured the British Youths title with rounds of 65, 74, 70, 69.

Those achievements earned Nick a scholarship at the University of Houston along with Sandy Lyle and Martin Poxon. But, like Lyle, he decided to return to Britain after only a few months as the academic side of the business bit into valuable practice time.

In the spring of 1976 Faldo ventured over the border to Scotland — a country with which he has had a peculiar love-hate relationship — and won the Craigmillar Park Open. As he admitted: 'The sensible thing to do then was turn professional.'

The fledgling pro took a creditable 58th place in the Order of Merit in 1976 with winnings of £2112, but a series of high finishes in 1977 carried him to eighth, £23,978 in official earnings, the Rookie of the Year award and, more importantly, a Ryder Cup berth.

Brian Huggett, the British and Irish captain at Royal Lytham in 1977, paired 20-year-old Nick with the experienced Peter Oosterhuis. It was a formidable-looking partnership (Oosterhuis 6ft 5in and Faldo 6ft 3in), and proved to be equally formidable in golfing terms.

The two golfing giants played together six times in Ryder Cup foursomes and fourballs, picking up four points. But in 1977 it was 'rookie' Faldo who ignited the experimental partnership.

Oosty recalled: 'The Ryder Cup is probably one of the most pressure-filled situations in professional golf, maybe more so than the "majors" because it's a different set of circumstances.

Although I knew Nick was a good player before Lytham, I didn't know how he would react to that situation.

'As it turned out, he coped extremely well and I quickly knew I could rely on his game. It was very solid right through and I think we soon built up a mutual respect.

'We beat Ray Floyd and Lou Graham 2 and 1 in the foursomes after being three or four down. Then in the fourballs we took on Floyd and Jack Nicklaus, which was a bigger challenge. Nick never flinched. We won 3 and 1 and everyone gave me credit for nursing him around — but in fact it was more the other way around.

'The wind was blowing like crazy and I was carving the ball off to the right. It was very difficult but Nick kept us in the game in the early holes before I picked up on the way home. Considering he was only 20, it was a very mature display.'

Faldo went on to complete an unforgettable Ryder Cup debut by beating Tom Watson — fresh from his Open success at Turnberry — in the singles to protect his 100% record. Ten years on, Nick was still upsetting Americans in the victorious 1987 match at Muirfield Village, accruing three and a half points out of five.

Suddenly Faldo was public property and he responded by giving the public what they wanted — a British golfer who seemed capable of emulating Tony Jacklin.

Nick had made a breakthrough of sorts by winning the 1977 Skol individual event at Gleneagles, the traditional 36-hole curtain-raiser for the now defunct Double Diamond team event. However, the following season he pulled off a much more significant victory.

Encouraged by a second place to Seve Ballesteros in the Martini International, Faldo shot 71, 68, 70, 69 over Royal Birkdale to claim the Colgate P.G.A. crown — a title he would regain at Sandwich in 1980, defend successfully at Ganton the following year, and win for a fourth time under Volvo's sponsorship at Wentworth in 1989.

The Haig Tournament Players Championship was the highlight of 1982 but no-one, not even Faldo, could have predicted his start to the 1983 season when, consecutively, he picked off the Paco Rabanne French Open, the Martini International and the Car Care Plan International.

In the Open at Birkdale Nick, having previously finished in the top dozen on four occasions, began encouragingly with a pair of 68s and a 71 before dropping away on the final afternoon with a closing 73 to finish joint eighth, just five behind Tom Watson. But at least it was a sign that he could withstand the stresses of life at the top of the leader board.

Further wins in the Lawrence Batley International and Ebel Swiss Open saw Faldo collect the Harry Vardon Trophy as leader of the European Order of Merit with £140,761. It was as well that he enjoyed those wins because the Car Care title in '84 and the Heritage Classic were to be the last victories for three years as Faldo underwent major surgery on that swing.

After the convalescence was completed at Muirfield in 1987, Nick tackled the major championships with unconcealed relish. Only five men played in all four rounds of all four 'majors' in 1988. Nick Faldo was one of them.

He shot 75, 74, 75, 72 to finish joint 30th in the Masters. Next came the U.S. Open at Brookline, Massachusetts, where rounds of 72, 67, 68, 71 hoisted Nick into an unsuccessful play-off with Curtis Strange. In the British Open at Royal Lytham, he was third to Seve Ballesteros after scores of 71, 69, 68, 71. Finally rounds of 67, 71, 70, 71 were good enough for fourth spot in the U.S.P.G.A.

Faldo had played the four biggest championships in a total of 1132 strokes, at an average of 70.75. Sadly, one of his weakest rounds was the 75 he carded in the play-off with Strange. The American coasted round in a level par 71 and Nick, not for the first time in 1988, finished second.

'On the day Curtis was better than me and it was as simple as that,' said Faldo. 'In the end I didn't put enough pressure on him. All he needed was a reasonable round and that's just what he managed to produce.'

Including that creditable second place, Nick was a 'bridesmaid' eight times in 1988 before a victory in the Volvo Masters in Spain at the end of the year forced him back into the winner's enclosure. The next time was to be at Augusta just over five months later.

Faldo arrived at the 53rd Masters in reasonable fettle, despite some modest finishes during his campaign in the States. He admitted: 'I'm swinging the club better than I've ever done. Basically my game is good but I do need a bit of luck, a few nice things to happen and yes, a bit of confidence'.

Four days later, in the fading light at Augusta's 10th hole, that vital slice of luck arrived. Scott Hoch hunched over a two-foot putt to win the Masters at the first hole of a play-off. Faldo watched impassively, arms folded, but inwardly seething after bunkering his second shot and taking a bogey five.

Back in the press interview room, Ben Crenshaw, watching on television, yelled: 'Jesus, hit it!' Still Hoch hesitated then earned miserable immortality by sending the ball past the hole. Faldo breathed in deeply and prepared to meet his destiny.

'It was at that moment that I knew I would win. Scott seemed to take forever over that putt. He looked like he was ready to go and then he hesitated and moved away. I knew what he was feeling. I knew it was for the Masters and I was aware that it was a tough thing to handle. The moment he missed that putt I knew he had let me in.'

Faldo strode purposefully to the 11th tee and found the centre of the fairway with his drive. He muttered to himself: 'Right, mate, go for it!' and drilled a No 3 iron 209 yards to within 25 feet of a hole which had cost him bogey fives in all four rounds.

Hoch pushed his approach wide of the green and chipped up short of the flag. Faldo sensed it was all over and seconds later the ball bolted into the hole, his triumphant pose a marked contrast to his crestfallen appearance earlier that same day.

Nick had shared the halfway lead with Lee Trevino after rounds of 68 and 73, but torrential rain forced the third round to be postponed. On the resumption the next morning, Faldo slumped to a five over par 77 and a tie for ninth place, five strokes behind Ben Crenshaw.

He retreated to his hotel for a few hours' relaxation and confessed: 'I sat there alone and quite despondent. Then, I don't know how it happened, I went from being negative to positive. I thought, I'm only five behind. That's all.

'The conditions were the best they had been all week. I was looking to play the last five holes in two under but instead I was two over. It moved me down the leader board so at lunch I had to settle myself down. I putted so poorly I knew I had to do something. I changed to a Taylor Made putter and finally found a stroke.'

The putts started to drop. Nick turned in 32, dropped the obligatory shot at the 11th, then birdied the 13th, 14th, 16th and 17th for a closing 65. Greg Norman and Ben Crenshaw both bogied the 18th to finish a stroke behind while hapless Hoch dropped into a tie of the lead at the 17th when he missed from two and a half feet. All that remained was a small matter of that play-off.

'Winning the Masters means the world to me,' Faldo confessed. 'Words don't describe a day like that. It is a dream come true and makes up for the U.S. Open. You see Jack Nicklaus shoot 65 on TV and think it's unbelievable. But when you do it, when you do something someone like Jack's done, you've holed a putt and the whole world's looking at you . . . it's unbelievable, it's ecstacy. I just want more of it.'

The victory lifted Faldo's U.S. winnings to $860,848 since 1981, but far more important was the knowledge that he had drawn level with Lyle. 'Now it's up to me to get ahead of him,' he added with a knowing smile.

CAREER RECORD

MAJOR TITLES: British Open 1987; U.S. Masters 1989.

OVERSEAS TITLES: ICL Tournament (South Africa) 1979; Paco Rabanne French Open 1983; Ebel Swiss Open 1983; Sea Pines Heritage Classic (USA) 1984; Peugeot Spanish Open 1987; Peugeot French Open 1988-89; Volvo Masters (Spain) 1988.

DOMESTIC TITLES: Skol Lager Individual Tournament 1977; Colgate P.G.A. 1978; Sun Alliance P.G.A. 1980-81; Haig Whisky TPC 1982; Martini International 1983; Car Care Plan International 1983-84; Lawrence Batley International 1983; Volvo P.G.A. 1989; Dunhill British Masters 1989.

INTERNATIONAL (Pro): Ryder Cup 1977-79-81-83-85-87-89; England in World Cup 1977; England in Double Diamond 1977; Hennessy Cognac Cup 1978-80-82-84; England in Dunhill Cup 1985-86-87-88; Nissan Cup 1986; Kirin Cup 1987.

AMATEUR: English Amateur 1975; British Youths 1975.

INTERNATIONAL (Amat): England Boys 1974; England Youths 1975; England in Home Internationals 1975; GB Commonwealth Team 1975.

MISC: Rookie of the Year 1977; Harry Vardon Trophy 1983; Braid Taylor Memorial Medal 1983 (jt) -84-87-88; Association of Golf Writers' Trophy 1983; Awarded MBE 1988.

10
SANDY LYLE

IT has been acclaimed as the greatest bunker shot in the history of golf. It was undeniably one of the most audacious strokes with which to capture a major championship. It also identified Sandy Lyle as a genuine global superstar.

Millions of sleepy Britons, who should have been safely tucked up in bed, sat spellbound in front of their television sets as the exhilarating climax to the 1988 U.S. Masters unfolded at Augusta National.

Across the Atlantic, Lyle ambled into a fairway bunker which had sucked in his No 1 iron tee shot at the 72nd hole. He needed a par four to force a play-off with Mark Calcavecchia; anything worse and the Masters green jacket would be draped around American shoulders yet again.

Of course, there was one other improbable alternative — a birdie three to win the title outright. But that, surely, was out of the question as Sandy planted his size twelve shoes in the sand and selected a No 7 iron for his second shot.

The next few seconds affected the outcome of the entire championship, but only Sandy Lyle can articulate the immense stress and mental turmoil he experienced in those mind-numbing moments.

'When I hit the No 1 iron off the 18th I knew I needed a par to force a play-off. My first thought was that the ball was okay but, as my reaction showed at the time — hopping from foot to foot — I quickly had the horrible feeling that it might land in the bunker.

'When the ball rolled into the sand I thought I could be in big trouble. The first bunker on the left is not the place to be because the ball can finish close to the face. Unfortunately, when you're thumping the ball around 250 yards it's pretty hard to judge where it lands to within four or five feet.

'As I walked up, I prayed that it had taken a soft bounce and not gone in too far. Luckily the ball had run into a position in the bunker where it lay slightly on the upslope. I had a clean lie and it was as if the ball was sitting on a launching pad.'

Although Sandy was relieved to find the lie to his liking, his problems were only just beginning.

'The club selection had to be right. I had to make sure I didn't catch the lip and I had to be certain I didn't take any sand along with the ball. If I had caught the sand at all, I would probably have lost, or at best made a pitch and putt four.

'Then again I could have knocked it into another bunker near the green and taken five or six which would have cost me the title. It had to be a 100% shot.

'I had 145 yards to go and took my seven iron. I picked it off the top of the sand just perfectly and the ball flew off the middle of the clubface. I knew instantly it was good.'

The ball soared onto the green, covering the flag all the way, and landing softly on the incline halfway up the two-tier green, 22 feet behind the hole. The pin was cut on the lower level and as Lyle listened anxiously for a tell-tale roar from the crowd, the TV viewers heard commentator Peter Alliss whisper: 'This could spin . . . this could spin.'

As if drawn by an invisible magnet, the ball slowly gathered momentum and trickled back down the slope to within 10 feet of the hole.

'I knew the ball had rolled back as soon as I heard the noise from around the green,' declared Sandy. 'I thought it would probably be about 15 feet away but it was nearer 10 and I had a holeable putt for victory.

'I expected the ball to keep to the right side, but I wanted to hit it fairly straight and at the correct pace. I didn't want to be short and I certainly didn't want to run it a few feet past and have that for a play-off!'

Lyle drew back his putter and made a sweet contact. The ball did drift slightly to the right but caught the rim and toppled in.

Sandy pummelled the air with two clenched fists and danced a spontaneous victory jig before resting his putter wearily on his right shoulder and heaving an enormous sigh of relief.

At the age of 30 years and two months, Sandy Lyle had become the first British golfer to capture the U.S. Masters, following in the illustrious footsteps of Sarazen, Snead, Hogan, Palmer and Nicklaus.

It was all a far cry from a seemingly insignificant moment at the climax of another major championship almost 21 years earlier at Royal Lytham and St. Anne's.

The occasion was the final round of the British Open and a small boy sitting in the vast grandstands towering over the 18th green shot out a chubby hand in a vain attempt to catch Tony Jacklin's golf ball.

Seconds earlier, Jacklin had ended 18 years of overseas domination in the Open by sinking the winning putt. Little Sandy Lyle missed the ball heaved high into the stands, but the emotional moment had made an indelible impression on his young mind.

'I recall sitting in the left-hand stand beside the last green. I was only four or five feet away from catching Tony's ball when he threw it into the crowd and I can remember thinking how nice it would be to play in that championship and win.'

Little did he know that when the Open returned to Lytham in 1974 he would, indeed, compete in the world's oldest championship — and survive the halfway cut as well.

The winning part came later.

But on that momentous July day in 1969, 11-year-old Sandy became hopelessly infatuated by golf. He told his dad of his ambition to become a professional . . . and father and son struck a bargain which drove the youngster towards his goal.

Alex Lyle, who moved from Glasgow to Shropshire in 1955 to become the pro at Hawkstone Park, explained: 'I remember Sandy returning from Lytham and chattering excitedly about the Open.

'All I heard was how wonderful Palmer and Nicklaus were and how he wanted to be like them. I told him that I would give him all the backing he needed to break into professional golf . . . if he could get down to scratch or plus one by the age of 15 or 16 and make the Walker Cup team.

'Until then he had been more interested in playing cowboys and indians than golf, but he was a thickset wee lad and could certainly knock the ball on quite well with an old wooden "baffie" which I cut down for him.

'At that point I insisted he join the golf club, but since there was no junior section he was playing against men immediately and, looking back, I feel that was no bad thing. He played for the county colts at 13 and the men's team at 14. He had a tremendous grounding with the county.'

Within a couple of months of joining Hawkstone Park, little 'Podge' or 'Fatty' Lyle, as he was known affectionately in the clubhouse, had reduced his handicap from 24 to 14 and never looked back. He also quickly shed his uncomplimentary nicknames.

'Sandy virtually grew up overnight,' recalled Alex Lyle. 'He was a porky wee boy but a dose of the measles kept him in bed for a week when he was 13. He just lay there, as red as a beetroot. When he got up he found his trousers were too short. He was a few inches taller, had lost a lot of weight around his waist, and suddenly wasn't a "fatty" any more.

'The one thing he has retained is his stockiness. He still has good shoulders and, most important of all, a tremendous pair of legs, which he uses to great effect.'

By the time Sandy was 14, his father faced an agonising decision. His son was showing immense promise and the amateur selectors were asking questions. Was Sandy, born in Shropshire of Glaswegian parents, eligible to represent England or Scotland?

The matter was finally and irrevocably resolved in 1977 when Lyle turned professional, but in 1972 there was no choice for Alex to make.

'I felt Sandy should play for England because he lived there and the county had been so good to him. I simply couldn't devote the time or the money to travel back and forth to Scotland.'

So Sandy Lyle tackled his amateur career as an Englishman and proceeded to carry all before him, much to the Scots' dismay — including some of the Lyle family living north of the border. Alex laughed: 'My brother-in-law was furious that Sandy was playing for England instead of Scotland.

'However, I'm absolutely positive we did the right thing. He had a top-class golfing education and he went right through all the grades. It's never an easy stepping stone, moving up from amateur to professional, but it helps greatly if you've come up that way.'

With the benefit of hindsight, Sandy feels his father made the correct choice. He said: 'It was only common sense that I played for England. I know it has caused a bit of a stir ever since, but dad was right. It would have been impossible to play in Scottish amateur events.'

Lyle's amateur career was nothing short of meteoric. He finished runner-up in the British Boys' Championship two years in a row, then graduated to youth level where he captured the British title in 1977.

In 1975, aged 16, he lifted the English Open Amateur stroke-play championship (Brabazon Trophy) from a field which included one Nicholas Faldo. Sandy regained that title in 1977 before turning professional.

All this time, Lyle was collecting international caps at boys, youths and senior levels and, in fact, he represented England at all three divisions in 1975.

Sandy also kept his side of that pact forged between father and son several years previously. At 15 he earned his scratch rating and became one of the elite amateurs the following year by being awarded a 'plus one' handicap.

The only outstanding part of the bargain was a Walker Cup place. He was duly selected for the match at Shinnecock Hills, New York, in August 1977 and after a rare disappointment — he lost all three games — decided the time was ripe to turn professional.

Once again the thorny issue of nationality came to the surface. Alex Lyle took up the story: 'It was Sandy's decision this time. He was an adult and a professional golfer so the reasons which applied in the early days didn't come into the argument.

'He took about three days to consider everything then he came down to breakfast one morning, looked at me and announced: "You are now talking to a Scotsman!" I have to admit I was delighted — but mainly because Sandy had made up his own mind.'

Certainly the American public seemed confused. Lyle's entry in the U.S.P.G.A. handbook described his birthplace as: 'Shrewsbury, Scotland'. However, Sandy remarked: 'When I turned professional I then had a choice. I opted for Scotland because my parents are very definitely Scottish and proud of it.

'Although I was born in England I am Scottish through and through. I know my accent doesn't help my claims to be a Scot but blood is a greater bond than an accent and I have been really well received in Scotland.'

Lyle went out of his way to emphasise the point when he returned to Augusta in 1989 to defend his Masters title. As champion, Sandy hosted, and paid for, the traditional dinner for those fortunate few who have earned the right to wear the coveted green jacket.

Not only did he arrive at the most famous inner sanctum in golf — the past champions' private locker room — resplendent in full highland dress, but insisted that haggis was included on the menu. The reaction of Ballesteros, Langer, Nicklaus and Co. when confronted with Scotland's aromatic delicacy is not recorded!

If Lyle's amateur career had taken off at breakneck speed, the transition to the upper echelons of the paid ranks was equally rapid.

He went to the P.G.A. school shortly after turning professional and promptly won it, earning his first pay cheque — £300. The ambitious youngster spent the winter under the tutelage of his father at Hawkstone Park before making his tournament debut in Nigeria at the start of 1978.

Sandy opened those powerful shoulders and scorched round in 61 and 63 in the first two rounds for a halfway total of 124, 18 under par. He admitted: 'I let things slip a bit after that and finished with rounds of 71 and 75. I tied with Michael King and beat him in the play-off so I didn't do too badly for my first event.'

By the end of his first full year 'on the road', Lyle had finished 49th in the European Order of Merit with £5234 and Henry Cotton's vote as Rookie of the Year. However, it was only a beginning.

The following summer saw Sandy Lyle emerge as more than just a raw-boned young man who smashed the ball prodigious distances. Inside that sturdy physique was someone who possessed the nerve, the temperament and the lightness of touch to reach the top.

Over the next two seasons Sandy took out a licence to print money, heading the Order of Merit in 1979 and '80 with winnings of just over £115,000 as well as a clutch of titles — the Jersey Open, the Scandinavian Enterprise Open, the European Open and the Coral Classic.

In those early days it was transparently obvious that Lyle was destined to be a dominant force on the European scene. But had he the ambition or the concentration to take on the world?

The misgivings were perfectly understandable. Sandy may have been studying a putt to win an important tournament, but to the observer he could just as easily have been playing for 50p in a Saturday morning fourball.

He had the discomfiting habit of missing shortish putts with reckless haste, and impressively low scores were apt to be followed by inexplicably high ones. However, Lyle hit back: 'It may look as if I don't care, but deep down, I do.'

Some of the doubts evaporated during the 1979 European Open at Turnberry, just a few days after he won the Scottish Professional Championship at Glasgow Gailes, where he disabused his critics of the notion that he was using Scotland as a flag of convenience.

Lyle tore Turnberry apart in the final round, birdieing six of the first seven holes on his way to a 65 and a seven-stroke win over Peter Townsend. It was an impressively mature performance by a 20-year-old and simply re-affirmed the enormous potential just waiting to be tapped.

Titles came thick and fast after that encouraging 1979 season: the French Open, the Lawrence Batley International (twice), the Madrid Open, Italian Open and Lancome Trophy. Then late in 1984 he devoured a world-class field to claim the Kapalua

International in Hawaii.

In the space of eight weeks Lyle won around £200,000 on three continents to prove his versatility. But still the uncertainty remained . . . until four unforgettable days on England's south coast at Sandwich in 1985.

'Winning the Open was not so much a dream as a gut feeling,' explained Sandy. 'It was something which crept up on me over the years and by the early eighties I felt it was only a matter of time until I won it.

'I had been finishing in the top 20 regularly and as I went through 1982, '83 and '84 I knew I had the golf to win an Open. However, I did have to cope with a lot of pressure because no British player had been successful since Tony Jacklin.'

Yet the build-up to Lyle's sublime triumph at Royal St. George's was scarcely designed to inspire confidence in an aspiring champion. Just a month before the Open, Sandy performed in a manner which would have shamed an 18-handicapper.

Competing — if that is the right word — in the first round of the storm-ravaged Carrolls Irish Open at Royal Dublin, Lyle came to the closing hole requiring a par four to break 90. He knocked his second shot out of bounds . . . and promptly quit.

'After three-putting the 17th to go 18 over par I knew I needed a par at the last to break 90 and decided to go for it, if only for my pride,' said Sandy. 'When I hit my second shot out of bounds, I'd had enough. I just picked up the ball and didn't return a card.'

Four weeks later, the same golfer was being fêted as the new Open champion, and as Lyle pointed out with a wry grin: 'It just goes to prove what a stupid game this is!

'Anyway, I went home to my dad to conduct the post mortem. There wasn't much time between the Irish Open and the British Open to sort things out but I'm lucky in that I can put things out of my mind very quickly.

'If I don't play well one week, it's forgotten almost as soon as I leave the course. There's always next week to concentrate on. As I say, it's lucky that I'm a laid-back kind of guy and didn't allow that dreadful performance to worry me. I reckoned there wasn't much wrong that my dad couldn't sort out. Quite honestly I think I was just tired and that caused my swing to get a little flat.'

By the time Lyle arrived at the vast sprawling south-coast links, he was driving well again and feeling quietly confident. It was not misplaced. As Alex Lyle says: 'When Sandy's down, he's dangerous!' And so it proved.

Lyle began his campaign with a two under par 68 which was good enough for a tie for second place, four shots behind leader Christy O'Connor Junior.

The middle two rounds are where most golfers jostle for position and Sandy's 71 and 73 carried him into a menacing position just three behind joint leaders David Graham and Bernhard Langer.

Lyle relaxed before the final round by playing with a set of Lego with his elder son, Stuart. But when the time came, he was ready to keep his appointment with destiny.

'I thought at the start of the final round I would have to make a 67 or 68 to have a good chance, but Bernard Gallacher assured me a 69 or 70 would do. He was right. A 70 was good enough.'

One by one the front runners surrendered as Lyle, after a bogey at the first, stayed calm and waited for his chance to pounce. It came at the long 14th.

'I bogeyed the 13th and felt a little dejected, but I knew I had to keep it going,' recalled Sandy. 'The key to my victory was undoubtedly the two shots I played at the 14th and 15th which set up birdies. At the 14th I drove into the rough and could only hit a sand wedge 80 yards.

'From there I hit a No 2 iron 220 yards to 45 feet and holed the putt for a birdie. Then at the 15th I hit a good drive and No 6 iron to 10 or 12 feet and holed that one as well. The putt on the 14th got things moving again but after the next one I knew I was in with a real shout.

'I thought to myself: "Three more pars might be enough" and fortunately my swing held up. I didn't feel jumpy at all over the last three holes. I was in control and got the club back without any shakes. I was thrilled to bits with myself.'

But the drama wasn't over yet. Sandy's No 6 iron second to the last drifted left and into thick, wiry rough in the little depression off the green known as Duncan's Hollow.

Lyle played his chip just too delicately — and the ball struggled to the top of the ridge running across the 18th green and rolled back down towards him. Sandy flopped to his knees and buried his head in his hands before getting down in two putts for a bogey five.

'Despite that look of despair when I sank to my knees, I knew I wasn't beaten. I had been told that Langer and Graham were in trouble at the 16th so I got the first putt reasonably close and made the second. At worst, I expected a play-off so I went to the recorder's tent and kept my concentration going in case I had to go out again.'

When Langer's desperate chip at the 18th stayed out, Lyle was the champion, Britain's first since Jacklin 16 years earlier, with a total of 282, one in front of American Payne Stewart.

With a replica of the Open trophy on his sideboard, a cheque for £65,000 in his pocket and the prospect of millions more to follow, Lyle wasted no time. America, the land of opportunity, was waiting to be conquered.

In 1986 he won the Greater Greensboro Open; in 1987 he captured the prestigious U.S. Tournament Players' Championship at Ponte Vedra and in 1988 would surely have become the first European to top the American money list but for his decision to return home.

The Phoenix Open fell to the big Scot who then became the first golfer in history to win at Greensboro before heading down to Georgia to annex the U.S. Masters among the floral splendour of Augusta National the following week. The Masters was his third American title in little over two months and Lyle eventually finished seventh behind Curtis Strange with a massive haul of $726,934.

'Winning the Open and the Masters gave me immense satisfaction, but for different reasons. Whereas the Open sort of crept up on me, I was in the lead at Augusta almost from the start. There was the pressure from the media and long, long rounds of 4 hours 50 minutes. It meant there was an awful lot of thinking going on out on the course. Too much, really, and it made great demands on your patience.'

However, patience, as Sandy has often remarked, is his 15th club and it was a quality which was tested to the limit at Augusta in 1988. After rounds of 71, 67 and 72 he stood at six under par, which represented a two-stroke lead over Calcavecchia and former winner Ben Crenshaw.

It is certainly a truism that the Masters doesn't start until the back nine on Sunday as Lyle discovered to his cost. The complexities of Amen Corner have haunted countless golfers down the years and Sandy was no exception.

With eight holes left, he was at eight under par and three in front of Calcavecchia and Craig Stadler. Three holes later he was a shot adrift.

After a bogey at the 11th he reached that peerless par three, Rae's Creek, which must be one of the most treacherous as well as picturesque short holes in championship golf.

'That was where I might have lost the Masters but didn't,' declared Sandy. 'I chose a No 8 iron and thought my shot was just right but it didn't carry far enough. Another six feet and it would have been perfect but it spun back into the water.

'I had to make a good pitch from 60 yards for my third and did well to escape with a five. That was a tremendous disappointment because I had had a special affinity with that hole over the years and, in fact, until that time I think I had played it in two under par.'

Suddenly Lyle's lead was wiped out and Calcavecchia's birdie at the long 13th propelled the American to the top of the leader board. The shift in fortunes may have looked ominous for Sandy, but it removed the strain of being in front for so long.

'I had been carrying that pressure for two days so I was a little relieved that somebody else had it. My caddie, Dave Musgrove, tried to keep me steady but he didn't have to. As I've said, I'm pretty level headed and just concentrated on unleashing a good solid drive at the 13th. I knew I was by no means out of it.'

Lyle failed to birdie the 13th or the other long hole, the 15th, but hit his No 7 iron — the club which he used to such lethal effect 30 minutes later — to 15 feet at the short 16th where he faced one of the slickest, trickiest putts on the course.

'The 16th was a crucial hole because of the difficulty of the putt. I knew when I lined up that I probably needed to make it — but there was a catch. If I missed the hole, the ball was guaranteed to run seven or eight feet past and that would have left me a return putt which would have been missable. Anyway, I read it properly and the ball disappeared. I was level again with Calcavecchia.'

All that was left was for Lyle to secure that breathtaking birdie at the last and allow Larry Mize to act as a valet while the first British winner of the U.S. Masters slipped on the coveted green jacket.

'Augusta was a fantastic breakthrough for me. The benefits are obvious. I get exemption for life there and it removes the worries of receiving invitations to return. I know I have at least six or seven more years to have another crack at winning the green jacket. I know now that I'm good enough to capture more major championships.

'That win was actually well received by the Americans. The people over there congratulated me on winning, as did those in charge at Augusta, even although they don't enjoy seeing their major titles disappear overseas.'

Twelve months later it was a different story as Sandy failed to make the halfway cut in the 1989 Masters. He was in exalted company, as Seve Ballesteros and Jack Nicklaus had both done the same thing in defence of the title, but it could not assuage the pain and embarrassment.

'I must be the worst defender of a major championship in the world,' groaned Lyle after rounds of 77 and 76 left him two strokes outside the cut. 'It was just as I feared; I've made a fool of myself.'

However, Sandy Lyle is nobody's fool. After his success at Augusta in 1988 he returned to Europe and added the Dunhill British Masters to his collection of 'masters' titles. Then, at long last, he captured the Suntory World Match-Play on the doorstep of his own mansion at Wentworth.

Four times in the previous eight championships Lyle had reached the final only to be edged out by Greg Norman twice, and Ballesteros and Ian Woosnam. At the fifth attempt he succeeded, with a 2 and 1 triumph over his old foe, Nick Faldo.

The event saw Lyle at his most imperial. He was a total of 25 under par for 99 holes of golf and in the final he extracted 12 birdies and an eagle from the Burma Road course. He reflected: 'Sometimes I wondered if I'd ever win this thing, but over the years I learned to avoid the destructive shots at Wentworth and to keep the ball in play.'

It was a glorious climax to a truly spectacular 1988 for Lyle. The victory, worth £75,000 hoisted his worldwide earnings for 12 calendar months beyond the $1 million mark while fifth place in the European Order of Merit took his total winnings in 10 seasons to £1,256,673 . . . second only to Ballesteros.

His start to 1989 was almost as impressive. Sandy played in five early-season events in the United States and amassed $269,845 after finishing runner-up twice and third once. However, a short break back in Britain cost him his momentum which he failed to recover for his Masters defence.

The incomparable Seve Ballesteros supplied the most fitting eulogy for Lyle after losing by the inconceivable margin of 7 and 6 in the semi-final of the 1988 World Match-Play. He commented: 'When Sandy's at his best he IS the best, but when he's bad he can be almost the worst.'

Infuriating he might be, but there are few dull moments when Sandy Lyle steps onto the golf course. And if anyone should need reminding of that fact, they should cast their minds back to Augusta '88, and to the bunker shot in a million.

CAREER RECORD
MAJOR TITLES: British Open 1985; U.S. Masters 1988.
OVERSEAS TITLES: Nigerian Open 1978; Scandinavian Enterprise Open 1979; French Open 1981; Madrid Open 1983; Italian Open 1984; Lancome Trophy (France) 1984; Kapalua International (Hawaii) 1984; Casio World Open (Japan) 1984; Greater Greensboro Open (USA) 1986-88; German Masters 1987; U.S. Tournament Players' Championship 1987; Phoenix Open (USA) 1988.
DOMESTIC TITLES: Jersey Open 1979; European Open 1979; Scottish P.G.A. 1979; Coral Welsh Classic 1980; Lawrence Batley International 1981-82; Benson and Hedges International 1985; Dunhill British Masters 1988; Suntory World Match-Play 1988.
INTERNATIONAL (Pro.): Ryder Cup 1979-81-83-85-87-89; Scotland in World Cup 1979-80-87; Hennessy Cognac Cup 1980-84; Scotland in Dunhill Cup 1985-86-87-88; Nissan Cup 1985-86; Kirin Cup 1987.
AMATEUR: English Open Amateur Stroke-Play 1975-77; British Youths 1977.
INTERNATIONAL (Amat.): England Boys 1972-73-74-75; England Youths 1975-76-77; England in Home Internationals 1975-76-77; GB Commonwealth Team 1975; GB v Europe 1976; England in European Team Championship 1977; Walker Cup 1977.
MISC: Rookie of the Year 1978; Harry Vardon Trophy 1979-80-85; Tooting Bec Cup 1982-88; Braid Taylor Memorial Medal 1985; Awarded MBE 1986; Association of Golf Writers' Trophy 1988.

11

IAN WOOSNAM

THERE are several agreeable ways of becoming a millionaire. Winning the football pools is one; claiming the family inheritance is another. Alternatively, you could play golf like Ian Woosnam for a year.

Woosnam is truly a man in a million. The chunky little Welshman amassed his fortune during 12 memorable months in 1987 which prompted a substantial revision of the record books. Not content with becoming the first golfer to bank £1 million in prize money in one year, he also scooped the first $1 million cheque in golf.

From the moment he captured the Hong Kong Open in the spring of 1987 (the first Briton to do so), Woosnam took out a licence to print money. He rampaged across four continents, smashing records indiscriminately. Titles were gathered as effortlessly as plucking the groceries from a supermarket shelf, and the cheques kept pouring in.

Midway through the year, a slightly bemused Woosnam reflected on his soaring fortunes and declared, perhaps a trifle optimistically: 'Now I want to be the best golfer in the world . . . and a millionaire by the time I'm 40!'

Little did he realise then that only five months later he would have fulfilled the latter part of his grandiose ambition with 11 years to spare, and divided the experts over the former.

Five victories in Europe were climaxed by his triumph over Sandy Lyle in the final of the Suntory World Match-Play Championship at Wentworth. As the first Briton to win that prestigious title and with a tidy sum of £439,075 in European earnings in his bank account, Ian could have put his feet up for the year. In fact he had barely started.

A month after taming Lyle and the famous Burma Road course in record-breaking fashion, 'Little Woosie' hopped on a plane to Hawaii with David Llewellyn, stashed away another $150,000 by helping Wales win the World Cup for the first time, then headed for South Africa.

Victory in the Sun City Classic, ahead of Nick Faldo, earned Woosnam a useful Christmas present of $1 million in the 'Winner Takes All' Tournament. Ian had set out in 1987 with the avowed intention of being recognised as the best golfer in Europe. Twelve months later he had the qualifications, if not the tangible evidence of a major title, to be considered the world leader that year.

'If anyone had told me at the start of the year what was to happen I wouldn't have believed them,' admitted Ian. 'It was just fantastic. I wouldn't have even believed it was possible.

'The Ryder Cup was the ultimate for me, beating the Americans on their own soil, but to win for Wales in the World Cup is a memory I'll always cherish. The whole year was a dream come true and I can't think of a better way of ending it than by winning a million dollars.'

The World Cup at Kapalua in Hawaii probably saw Woosnam reach the zenith of his considerable physical and mental powers during that unforgettable season. By then nothing seemed impossible. He was neither intimidated nor perturbed by the course, the climate or the competition.

David Llewellyn, who partnered Woosman, carded a four-round total of 300 — the highest score among the top 10 nations in the finishing order — yet still pocketed a cheque for $100,000. It was Woosie who delivered the virtuoso performance.

In howling winds and biting rain, the pocket-sized Welshman gouged out rounds of 67, 70, 65, 72 for a 14 under par total of 274. It was enough to secure the $50,000 individual title — but national pride mattered more.

After tying with Scotland's Sandy Lyle and Sam Torrance, Wales claimed their first World Cup at the second hole of a play-off when 1985 Ryder Cup hero Torrance three-putted.

Llewellyn believes that his partner's performance that week has never been equalled. It sounds like an outrageous, jingoistic claim but he insisted: 'I don't think anyone has hit more pure golf shots than Ian did in those four days. He had to be the best player in the world at that moment.

'Considering the conditions, I would say those four rounds were the best golf anyone's ever played. I mean the best anywhere. God, the winds were howling at 40 miles an hour and it was raining heavily. In terms of quality play, I don't think it has ever been surpassed.'

To Llewellyn, it was a feat of epic proportions. To Woosnam, it was all in a week's work — another $150,000 to swell the coffers; another two titles (team and individual); another confident step up the ladder towards true golfing greatness.

The statistics, not always the most reliable of guides, can provide some sort of indication of the Welshman's bewitching performances in 1987. In Europe alone, Ian's then record total of £439,075 was £14,030 more than he had amassed in his previous nine gruelling seasons on the Tour.

In 21 Order of Merit tournaments he finished 'in the money' 19 times; in the top 10 a total of 13 times. He was a collective 157 under par (only twice over it in 72-hole events) and had a stroke average of 69.81. If that sounds impressive, his 22nd and last European appearance in the Suntory World Match-Play saw Woosnam destroy all challengers, and storm-ravaged Wentworth, with figures of 32 under par for his four ties.

Seve Ballesteros could only shake his head in disbelief that this stocky little character could bludgeon the ball such prodigious distances and summon up such a stunning variety of golf shots.

'When little Ian grows up he will be a great player,' declared Seve with a wicked grin. Ian also smiled at the joke. He could afford to, since in golfing terms he was the person who had walked tall in 1987.

Size was never regarded as a disadvantage by Woosnam. In fact, his diminutive appearance worked in his favour as it ensured that he became imbued with the little man's burning desire to topple the bigger guy. Ian may sometimes appear a physical midget alongside Greg Norman or Andy Bean, but as the latter found to his cost in the 1987 Ryder Cup, golfing prowess owes more to talent and tempo than a Charles Atlas physique.

Although lacking in stature, Woosnam has never been short of muscle-power, a legacy from his childhood on his father's 70-acre farm near Oswestry close to the English-Welsh border.

Despite the geographical quirk which could have made him eligible to represent England or Wales, Woosnam was never ambiguous about his nationality. He was Welsh — and proud of it. He remarked: 'Both my parents are Welsh and I learned my golf on the local Llanymynech course which has 15 holes in Wales and three in England. I also played for Wales as an amateur — and my heroes were always Brian Huggett and Dai Rees.'

From the age of seven — when he first swung a golf club — Ian rose at 5am, milked and fed the cows, then walked three miles to school. But his powerful forearms came from driving the tractor around Harold Woosnam's farm. The vehicles then had no power steering and his arms had to do all the work.

'I mucked in on the farm when I was a kid,' admitted Ian. 'But it wasn't the life for me. It was too much like hard work.' Hard work maybe, but vital to the Woosie success story in later years.

Unlike his Shropshire county team-mate, Sandy Lyle, who enjoyed the benefit of rudimentary grounding in the game from his professional father, young Woosnam simply padded around behind his 'old man', attempting to knock the cover off the ball.

'I've always believed you should hit the ball as far as you possibly can to start off with then start straightening it up. If you hit it short and then try to hit it further, it's a very difficult thing to do.

'I'm self-taught really. I did have a couple of lessons off an old guy, Cyril Hughes, who used to play in the days of Henry Cotton but he just taught me the basics. Because I'm small, it's natural for me to swing the way I do.'

Woosnam reduced his handicap to six by the age of 13. Three years later he left school with two O levels to join the greenkeeping staff of the Hill Valley club near Whitchurch before turning professional in September, 1976, aged 18, with a handicap of one and limited prospects.

Three times he attempted to qualify for his 'card' at the European Tour's players' school at Foxhills. He finally succeeded and so began the long, soul-destroying grind of travelling the length and breadth of Europe in search of his fortune.

'My dad told me it would be tough trying to make the grade as a professional, but I didn't realise how tough. For years I had to do part-time work as a barman and a labourer to make ends meet.

'I drove from tournament to tournament in a beat-up old caravanette and slept in the back because I couldn't afford to join the rest of the lads in hotels. I felt rich with thirty quid in my pocket.'

Ian 'dined' —if that's the right word — on a monotonous diet of crisps, soup and tins of baked beans. He joked: 'There were nights when a plate of fish and chips was a real luxury!

'I once drove from Inverness to Milan in three days. On the trip the caravanette broke down. The only way I could pay the garage bill was to finish in the top 10 in the Italian Open. I finished ninth.'

Those days of scratching together enough money to effect running repairs on the van, eating injudiciously and playing indifferently, began to demoralise Woosnam. He had given himself five years to make the grade and the indications were that he would fail. An encouraging 1980 season, in which he won £3481 and finished 87th on the money list, had given way to an inept 1981 — only £1884 to show for life on the treadmill. His spirit was almost broken . . . but not quite.

'I had got down to the stage where I was going to apply for a job at Oswestry Golf Club,' he confessed. 'I would walk off the course and think: "I'm never playing golf again". Then a few days later I'd be alright. I'd just get over the frustration.

'But it's so difficult. You've no money and you're slogging away. You can't really do it right. You play a couple of tournaments and then you have to do some work to make money. I think I've always been motivated by money because I needed it, you know.'

By the start of 1982, Ian was in a mood of black despair. In four seasons on the European Tour he had earned barely £6500 and had lurched to 104th in the Order of Merit. The future looked distinctly bleak.

Then came the turning point. He said: 'I found a sponsor in 1982. It took the pressure off a little bit. I knew that if I didn't win any money one week I'd be alright the next. The more money I had, the better I played.'

The prospect of another year of pre-qualifying didn't appeal to the frustrated young pro, but Ian knew there was one final chance to pick up an exemption . . . by finishing in the top three on the Safari Tour money list.

Woosnam decided it was time to grasp the nettle. He didn't win in Africa, but only lost out in a play-off with David Jagger for the Nigerian Open, and his consistency on the Dark Continent earned him that precious third place with winnings of £13,970.

With the burden of pre-qualifying lifted from his shoulders, Ian went from strength to strength, finishing joint runner-up in the Italian Open, Benson and Hedges International and the Spanish Open. But it was high in the Swiss Alps at Crans-sur-Sierre that he made the all-important breakthrough.

Woosnam fired rounds of 68, 68, 66, 70 to tie with Bill Longmuir, then beat the Scot at the third extra hole to lift the biggest cheque of his career, £10,085. It hardly compared with his $1 million prize at Sun City five years later, but at the time it felt like a million pounds.

Two months later the rejuvenated Welshman added the Cacharel World Under-25 Championship and another £3300 to his expanding bank balance. He was eighth in the Order of Merit with £48,794 at the end of the year. Ian Woosnam had arrived.

From that moment there was no stopping the pugnacious little Welsh fighter. His 1983 season was climaxed by a victory on home soil at St. Pierre when he won the Silk Cut masters with four sub-70 rounds to collect £16,600 and secure a Ryder Cup debut in Florida.

That same year Woosnam married his childhood sweetheart, Glendryth, who had also been born in the small village of St. Martins just three miles outside the Welsh border where Ian made his first appearance in the world.

Victory in the Scandinavian Enterprise Open and sixth place in the Order of Merit encouraged the impression that Woosnam might yet live up to the prediction of his fellow countryman Huggett, who had said years earlier that the little man affectionately named 'the toy bulldog' was a potential champion.

Despite drawing a blank in title terms in 1985, Ian passed the six-figure mark in official winnings, achieving his highest finish — fourth — in the Order of Merit and holding onto that position the following season.

In the Peugeot French Open in 1986, Woosnam set a P.G.A. European Tour record he would rather forget — by running up a 16 at the par three third hole at La Boulie in Paris. Not surprisingly, he missed the cut with a second round 81 and he said sheepishly: 'I had six putts and eight penalty strokes for hitting the ball while it was moving!'

But it was the 115th Open Championship at Turnberry which brought Woosnam to the attention of a larger audience. Only one player matched Turnberry's difficult par of 70 in the first round in gruesome conditions, and Ian achieved it with an aching back.

He said at the time: 'I've suffered from a bad back for months but I would have played in the Open on one leg if necessary. I wouldn't miss this championship for the world.'

Further rounds of 74, 70 and 72 were sufficient to earn Woosnam a share of third place with Bernhard Langer, but his problems in the lumbar region did little to help his cause. Like many leading professionals — Jack Nicklaus and Seve Ballesteros are the most notable examples — Woosnam is plagued by chronic back pains.

The great Henry Cotton suffered from a deformity of the spinal column due to endless hours of practice as a young man, and Ian discovered he had a slight curvature of the spine — caused, he surmises, by the strenuous work he did around his father's farm.

'Not only that, but hours of golf practice puts a strain on the back, particularly putting. In the last few years I've spent a lot of time on the putting green, and being all cramped up doesn't help.'

Over the years Ian took painkiller and anti-inflammatory pills to help him complete pain-wracked rounds. He experimented with various forms of fringe medicine: acupuncture, osteopathy, herbal remedies and faith healing. Then in March 1987, the problem was diagnosed.

'I went to see a doctor about the backache, which had been bothering me for about 10 years. I was told it was a form of spondylitis and the doctor sent me for a scan, but the back was okay and hadn't got any worse in the 10 years.

'I was so tense that, when I had an early morning start, I had to get up very early so that I could loosen up as I was so stiff. The doctor told me to do plenty of exercises and gave me muscle relaxant pills. They've worked a treat. I try not to take too many but now I wake up and am feeling loose and absolutely ready for work.'

It was late September of 1986 before Woosnam resumed his winning ways, capturing the Lawrence Batley Tournament Players' Championship at The Belfry — the course where he and Paul Way had teamed up to beat Hubert Green and Fuzzy Zoeller on consecutive days to help Europe's historic Ryder Cup success in 1985.

After two rounds of 71, Ian was infuriated by his inability to score. He admitted: 'Then I suddenly had a flash of inspiration after 11 holes of the third round. I'd been depressed and frustrated over my putting and in desperation I switched to a method I'd been experimenting with — lining the putter up square to the hole from behind then moving round to the normal address position without altering anything.

'I discovered that I'd been aiming to the right all the time. Suddenly all the putts started dropping,' added Ian, who surged through the field with scores of 66 and 69 to win his first title in Britain for two years.

When 1987 dawned, Woosnam felt ready to take on the world. He was already a cult figure in Europe on account of the awesome strength, which constantly defied logical explanation, inside that pocket-sized frame. He was the type of cuddly character who could have charmed the Americans . . . if he had been permitted.

Despite his prominent showings in two Ryder Cups and fourth position in the European money list two years in a row, Ian was snubbed by the organisers of the U.S. Masters. It was just the sort of attitude which infuriated the temperamental Welshman.

'Just what do I have to do to get an invitation?' he demanded to know. 'The event is ranked as one of the world's four majors, should have a world-class field, and I feel that I should be there. I want to prove to the world that I can perform on any stage.'

While his contemporaries Lyle and Faldo were performing at Augusta National, Woosnam carried his grudge around the European circuit and proceeded to win the Jersey

Open (–9), the Madrid Open (–19), the Bell's Scottish Open (–20) and Lancome Trophy (–24) . . . a staggering 72 under par in four title wins.

By the time he arrived at Wentworth in October, Ian had enhanced his reputation still further by partnering Nick Faldo to three and a half points out of four in the triumphant Ryder Cup match at Muirfield Village. He was indisputably No 1 in Europe, but the World Match-Play was traditionally a harbinger of doom for British players, none of whom had won in 23 attempts.

Woosnam was to change that. He still needed to silence the critics who were unable to accept that he had become one of the world's leading players. With wins over American Sam Randolph, Nick Faldo, Seve Ballesteros and Sandy Lyle, he succeeded admirably.

Ian condemned Lyle to his fourth defeat in the final, which ended at the 36th hole. The players had exchanged 18 birdies and an eagle before Woosnam sank his six-foot birdie attempt at the last to secure the £75,000 winner's cheque.

'I wasn't even nervous. I knew I could hole it because I'd holed putts of much the same line and length in my previous matches against Nick and Seve. I knew I could hole it because I'd done it before.'

Woosie's near-flawless performance inspired Ballesteros to make his humorous jibe about the Welshman's height. Lyle responded: 'I hope he doesn't grow up. He'll hit the ball 2000 miles if he does!'

If Woosnam had carried all before him, it appeared that he was carrying the weight of the world on his shoulders for a considerable part of 1988. Ian had signed a seven-figure contract to play with a set of Japanese clubs and spent months of torment grappling with his unfamiliar new tools before finally altering them.

A reaction to his 1987 success had been anticipated, but not a collapse of such epic proportions. He seldom threatened to make the halfway cut, far less win tournaments. Even Jack Nicklaus threw in his tuppenceworth at the American T.P.C. event by advising him: 'Forget the season completely.'

Woosnam stuttered from one disaster to another but hoped to change his luck with another visit to the United States, where his wish to play in the Masters had been granted. It was a futile exercise as he missed the cut. The insatiable media probed deeper. Were the new clubs responsible? Was it too much golf? Was Woosie cashing in on his '87 success instead of focusing clearly on winning tournaments?

The truth is probably a combination of all those circumstances. At the time, Woosnam mused: 'I should have tried the clubs out before signing anything. All they did was ruin my self-confidence. At the start of the year I felt as if I could play with a stick and win. Now I'm not looking forward to anything, although I think I have the clubs right at last.'

In any case, it was all hypothetical as Ian finally returned to the winner's enclosure by collecting the Volvo P.G.A. Championship at Wentworth in late May. The previous week he had shot four sub-70 rounds to finish tied sixth in the Italian Open and admitted: 'I was looking forward to this week. I was practising so hard my hands were bleeding.'

The rehabilitation was complete a couple of months later with a runaway seven-stroke victory in the Carrolls Irish Open at Portmarnock followed by a three-shot win in the Panasonic European Open at Sunningdale — just a week after a second-place finish in the Ebel Swiss Open lifted his career winnings in Europe over the £1 million threshold.

'It was hell at the start of that season. You start to wonder if things will ever improve. It's all about bloody hard work. There are no shortcuts. Victories in the Volvo P.G.A. and the Carrolls proved that 1987 was not a fluke. Nobody can call me a one-season wonder. I am a damn good player.'

Woosnam's luck in the major championships deserted him in 1988. After missing the Masters cut due to his miserable form, he injured wrist ligaments in a fall from his son's toy bike and scratched from the U.S. Open. The problem healed in time for him to finish joint 25th in the British Open at Royal Lytham before he withdrew from the U.S.P.G.A. after an opening 78.

In spite of the early-season traumas, Woosnam still managed to finish his European commitments in fourth place with earnings of £270,674. However, the horizon was clouded by the fact that a first 'major' had eluded him.

The 1989 U.S. Masters hinted that the task was not beyond him. After missing the 36-hole cut the previous year, Ian returned to Augusta National and occupied 14th place with three others to secure an invitation from Hord Hardin and his committee in 1990.

Two months later Woosnam reaffirmed the impression that the big breakthrough was just around the corner. The old verve and flair of the vintage 1987 season came flooding back as Ian claimed a share of second place on his first visit to the U.S. Open.

The demanding Oak Hill course in upstate New York held no fears for the Welshman who upstaged all but Curtis Strange with four finely crafted rounds of 70, 68, 73 and 68.

Woosman's final score of 279 was just one too many to force a play-off with the American, but a cheque for £44,000 eased the disappointment.

The battered old caravanette has been replaced by the trappings of success. A gleaming Porsche with a personalised number plate and a Mercedes sit in the driveway of his beautiful home in Oswestry, but that major title remains his ultimate dream.

'My performances in 1987 made me secure for life, so I now have the advantage of not having to think money. One of my goals was to become a millionaire out of golf. I've done that now so my only goal is to win a major.'

Life has changed greatly for Ian Woosnam since the day in 1970 when Sandy Lyle beat the tiny tot in the Shropshire and Herefordshire Boys' Championship.

'I'll get you yet,' muttered the angelic-looking little Welshman. Woosnam certainly did just that in the Suntory World Match-Play final in 1987. Now the big time really beckons.

CAREER RECORD
OVERSEAS TITLES: Swiss Open 1982; Cacharel World Under-25 Championship 1982;

Scandinavian Enterprise Open 1984; Zambian Open 1985; '555' Kenya Open 1986; Hong Kong Open 1987; Cepsa Madrid Open 1987; Lancome Trophy 1987; World Cup Individual 1987; Sun City Classic (South Africa) 1987.

DOMESTIC TITLES: Silk Cut Masters 1983; Lawrence Batley Tournament Players' Championship 1986; Jersey Open 1987; Bell's Scottish Open 1987; Suntory World Match-Play Championship 1987; Volvo P.G.A. Championship 1988; Carrolls Irish Open 1988-89; Panasonic European Open 1988.

INTERNATIONAL (Pro.): Ryder Cup 1983-85-87-89; Hennessy Cognac Cup 1982-84; Wales in World Cup 1980-82-83-84-85-87; Wales in Dunhill Cup 1985-86-88; Nissan Cup 1985-86; Kirin Cup 1987.

INTERNATIONAL (amat.): Wales (v France) 1976.

MISC: Harry Vardon Trophy 1987.